Study Guide

for use with

We the People

Fourth Edition

Thomas E. Patterson
Harvard University

Prepared by
Willoughby Jarrell
Kennesaw State University

Boston   Burr Ridge, IL   Dubuque, IA   Madison, WI   New York   San Francisco   St. Louis
Bangkok   Bogotá   Caracas   Lisbon   London   Madrid
Mexico City   Milan   New Delhi   Seoul   Singapore   Sydney   Taipei   Toronto

McGraw-Hill Higher Education

A Division of The **McGraw-Hill** *Companies*

Study Guide for use with
WE THE PEOPLE, FOURTH EDITION.
THOMAS E. PATTERSON.

Published by McGraw-Hill Higher Education, an imprint of The McGraw-Hill Companies, Inc., 1221 Avenue of the Americas, New York, NY 10020. Copyright © The McGraw-Hill Companies, Inc., 2002, 2000. All rights reserved.

This book is printed on acid-free paper.

1 2 3 4 5 6 7 8 9 0 QPD QPD 0 3 2 1

ISBN 0-07-245601-9

www.mhhe.com

TABLE OF CONTENTS

CHAPTER ONE
- THE AMERICAN HERITAGE -

LEARNING OBJECTIVES

After reading this chapter students should be able to

1. Identify the core ideals that constitute American political culture.
2. Discuss the importance of these ideals to American political culture as well as the reasons these ideals do not match the reality of people's experiences.
3. Identify the roots of political conflict.
4. Define the terms and discuss the relationships among power, authority and policy.
5. Define the terms constitutionalism, capitalism and democracy and discuss how they act as rules to guide the play of politics in the United States.
6. Distinguish among majoritarian, pluralist and elitist theories of power.
7. Explain the "political system" model.

FOCUS AND MAIN POINTS

This chapter explains and puts into historical perspective the principles that have shaped American politics since the nation's earliest years. It explores the power and limits of these principles. Students are introduced to concepts that influence policymaking choices, including constitutionalism, democracy, capitalism, power and authority. At the end of the chapter, the "political system" explanatory model is used to provide a framework that illustrates the workings of government and to introduce the topics covered in subsequent chapters. The main points covered in this chapter are the following:

- American political culture centers on a set of core ideals--liberty, equality, self-government, individualism, diversity and unity--that serve as the people's common bond.

- Politics is the process that determines whose values will prevail in society. The play of politics in the United States takes place in the context of democratic procedures, constitutionalism and capitalism, and involves elements of majority, pluralist and elite rule.

- Politics in the United States is characterized by a number of major patterns, including a highly fragmented governing system, a high degree of pluralism, an extraordinary emphasis on individual rights and a pronounced separation of the political and economic spheres.

CHAPTER SUMMARY

The United States is a nation that was formed on a set of ideals that include liberty, equality, self-government, individualism, diversity and unity. These ideals became Americans' common bond and today are the basis of their political culture. Although they are mythic, inexact and conflicting, these ideals have had a powerful effect on what generation after generation of Americans have tried to achieve politically for themselves and others.

Politics is the process by which it is determined whose values will prevail in society. The basis of politics is conflict over scarce resources and competing values. Those who have power win out in this conflict and are able to control governing authority and policy choices. In the case of the United States, no one faction controls all power and policy. Majorities govern on some issues, while groups and elites each govern on other issues.

The play of politics in the United States takes place through rules of the game, which include democracy, constitutionalism and capitalism. Democracy is rule by the people, which, in practice, refers to a representative system of government in which the people rule through their elected officials. Constitutionalism refers to rules that limit the rightful power of government over citizens. Capitalism is an economic system based on a free market principle that allows the government only a limited role in determining how economic costs and benefits will be allocated.

The political system model is a useful tool for instructional purposes that emphasizes the interrelated aspects of the actual workings of government. The model is based on demand and support inputs, the institutions of government, and outputs which are the public policy decisions that are binding on society.

MAJOR CONCEPTS

authority--the recognized right of an official or institution to exercise power.

capitalism--an economic system based on the idea that government should interfere with economic transactions as little as possible. Free enterprise and self-reliance are the collective and individual principles that underpin capitalism.

constitutionalism--the idea that there are definable limits on the rightful power of a government over its citizens.

democracy--a form of government in which the people govern, either directly or through elected representatives.

diversity--the principle that individual differences should be respected, are a legitimate basis of self-interest and are a source of strength for the American nation.

2

elitism--the view that the United States is essentially run by a tiny elite (composed of wealthy or well-connected individuals) who control public policy through both direct and indirect means.

equality--the principle that all individuals have moral worth and are entitled to fair treatment under the law.

government--the effort of people to find agreeable ways of living together.

individualism--a philosophical belief that stresses the values of hard work and self-reliance and holds that individuals should be left to succeed or fail on their own.

liberty--the principle that individuals should be free to act and think as they choose provided they do not infringe unreasonably on the freedom and well-being of others.

majoritarianism--the idea that the majority prevails not only in elections but also in determining policy.

pluralism--a theory of American politics which holds that society's interests are substantially represented through the activities of groups.

policy--generally, any broad course of governmental action; more narrowly, a specific government program or initiative.

political culture--the characteristic and deep-seated beliefs of a particular people.

political system--the various components of American government constitute a political system. The parts are separate but they connect with each other, affecting how each performs.

politics--the process through which society makes its governing decisions.

power--the ability of persons or institutions to control policy.

self-government--the principle that the people are the ultimate source and proper beneficiary of governing authority; in practice, a government based on majority rule.

unity--the principle that Americans are one people who form an indivisible union.

BOXES, TABLES AND FIGURES IN THE TEXT

INSTRUCTIONS FOR READING CHARTS, GRAPHS AND FIGURES

The text includes a wide array of graphs, tables, figures, charts, and maps that can present information pictorially or show how something has changed over time. A graphic portrayal of information can provide a lot of data in a space efficient manner and can clarify complex relationships among data. It is easy to learn how to interpret graphic information by following the instructions given below. Chapter One contains a map (p. 4) and a bar graph (p. 7) which will be used to illustrate basic instructions for reading them.

- Find the title of the graph. The title for the map in Figure 1-1 in Chapter One (p. 4) is "Total Immigration to the United States, 1820-1998, by Continent and Country of Origin." The bar graph on p. 7 does not have a title next to the illustration which means that one must look closely in the text to find out what the graph is illustrating. The bar graph illustrates the percentages of respondents from several nations who agreed with the statement "success in life is pretty much determined by forces outside our control."

- Next, look at the numbers on the graph to find out what they represent. The clues for telling you this are somewhere on the graph or in the explanation below the title of the figure. The information in Figure 1-1 is contained in separate boxes by continent. Arrows point to where on the map the countries listed under the continents are located. The bar graph in the box on page 7 illustrates that 69% of people from Italy (the tallest bar on the far right of the graph) agreed with the statement "success in life is pretty much determined by forces outside our control," which is a higher percentage than people in the United States (the shortest bar on the far left of the graph, representing 43%). If a person had merely glanced at the title of the box "Capitalism, Self-Reliance, and Personal Success" and then to the graph without looking closely at what is being measured, one could mistakenly surmise that the United States was low in support of capitalism, self-reliance and personal success. Try your skills out on the bar graph at the top of p. 19.

- Look for the point the graph is making. The point Figure 1-1 makes is right underneath the title of it. It tells you that America is a nation of immigrants who are joined together through a common set of ideals. The point the graph on page 7 makes is summarized in the sentence just above the bar graph, which states "The percentage of Americans and Europeans agreeing with the statement are shown in the accompanying chart."

- Ask yourself what the importance or lasting significance is of the point the graph is making. For instance, in Figure 1-1, by looking in the names of countries in the boxes and the figures of immigrants from each country, one can clearly see that a great deal of immigration has come from Europe as compared with Asia and the Americas. This can be contrasted with immigration from Oceania and Africa. The total number of immigrants is summarized at the top of each box by the region of the world. The total for Europe is 36.9 million immigrants and within Europe the total from Germany is 7.0 million. Similarly, the bar graph on p. 7 illustrates the point that differences between American and European cultures is reflected in their differing political traditions.

- Look for the sources for information presented on tables or figures. This is usually at the bottom of the figure if the information came from a source other than the author of your text. The information for Figure 1-1 came from the U.S. Immigration and Naturalization Service. The source for information contained in the bar graph in the box on "How the United States Compares" (p. 7) is found in the text of the box. It came from a survey done by Times-Mirror.

- Lastly, check your text again to see which paragraphs or portions the graph is helping to illustrate. A reference to Figure 1-1 is on p. 3 of the text while the reference to the bar graph and box on "How the United States Compares" can be found on page 6 of the text.

INTERNET RESOURCES

The web site for the Patterson text offers instructors and students up-to-date information on American politics that is keyed to the text's chapters. This site is located at: http://www.mhcollege.com/social/poli/patterson/htm.

Information about political science teaching and research can be found by joining a list using your institution's main computers along with the appropriate account for using that computer system. To subscribe to a list, send a message "listserv@*location-of-list* " with instructions "subscribe*LISTNAMEyourname*". The particular list you are seeking is Psrt-l@mizzou1.missouri.edu.

The American Political Science Association maintains an information service though Gopher. It provides information organized by the major sub-fields of the discipline as well as a list of lists pertaining to political science, conference information and a wealth of information about the three branches of government. It can be accessed at Gopher: //apsa.trenton.edu:70/.

The Library of Congress can be accessed through Gopher or the World-Wide Web. Through it you can locate political documents including treaties and the *Federal Register*. Access it on the web through: http://www.loc.gov/.

Information on major political theorists can be located on the web at: http://swift.eng.ox.ac.uk/jdr/index.html.

Information about worldwide democratic movements can be obtained through http://www.auburn.edu/tann/.

A site dedicated to American political culture including a summary of a comprehensive survey of Americans' cultural opinions is located at: http://minerva.acc.virginia.edu/~postmod

For the latest political news from leading news organizations, including the Washington Post see: http://www.politicsnow.com

Information about Alexis de Tocqueville including biographical, his writings, and references can be found at: http://www.tocqueville.org

ANALYTICAL THINKING EXERCISE

It is especially important to develop analytical thinking and evaluation skills when confronting issues, events and personalities in the political world. Basic tools for analytical thinking can be learned and practiced by applying them to materials in your text.

Read the inaugural address by George W. Bush at the end of Chapter One. Note down and list the major points made in each paragraph of the address. Summarize the main point the author is making in the speech. Then, ask yourself the following questions about the speech:

a) Can you discern a particular point of view or value that the author of the speech wants to convey?

b) What evidence, data or arguments does the author present to either illustrate the thesis of the speech or support the important points made in the speech?

c) What was the most convincing part of the speech for you? Least convincing?

d) Are the arguments (or points) in the speech presented logically? Do they make inappropriate links between cause and effect? See if they fall prey to typical logical fallacies such as attributing that something is the cause of something that follows it simply because it preceded it in time; finding that a speaker or writer attacks the individual, making an assertion rather than confronting the argument itself; begging the question by making a conclusion from an unfounded premise; generalizing improperly from a special case to a general rule. These are just a few common fallacies.

e) Is the author of the speech guilty of stereotyping groups, ethnocentrism, use of emotionalism or propagandistic techniques?

f) How did the essay support material presented in the chapter? Are there any challenges to the material presented in the chapter?

g) What new vocabulary did you learn from the speech?

h) Describe your own position on the topic presented in the speech. Has your position been altered as a result of reading the speech?

Note: for subsequent readings in the text substitute "essay" for "speech" when applying the critical thinking format.

TEST QUESTIONS FOR REVIEW

True/False

1. Americans prefer for wealth to be allocated by government direction and control rather than through the marketplace.

2. Compared with European democracies, Americans show a weak commitment to equality and social welfare programs.

3. A major characteristic of the American political system is its extraordinary emphasis on individual rights.

4. The concept of constitutionalism allows for some restrictions to be put on the exercise of individual rights.

5. Americans practice democracy by using the representative model rather than by direct rule.

6. In American society, political conflict can occur over scarcity of resources and access to a guaranteed minimum standard of living.

7. Equality of opportunity is not an important concept in the United States.

8. The United States has one of the most costly and elaborate sets of programs for the poor and disadvantaged of any of the industrialized democracies.

9. Unity is the principle that Americans should be free to act and think as they choose.

10. The United States has the world's most elite system of college education.

Multiple Choice

1. The American national identity has been most strongly affected by common:
a. ethnicity.
b. religious beliefs.
c. political beliefs.
d. class consciousness.

2. Politics is described as the process that:
a. inculcates deep beliefs in idealized form.
b. gives people economic equality.
c. applies power fairly.
d. determines whose values will prevail in society.
e. provides for respect of individual differences.

3. Major patterns that characterize politics in the United States include all except which one of the following:
a. a highly fragmented governing system.
b. little or no confidence in capitalism.
c. a high degree of pluralism.
d. extraordinary emphasis on individual rights.
e. pronounced separation of the political and economic spheres.

4. The American political culture contains which of the following ideals:
1. liberty
2. equality
3. diversity
4. unity
5. self-government
a. 1 and 3.   b. 1, 3, 5.   c. 1, 2, 4.   d. 1, 2, 3, 4.   e. all the above.

5. Cultural beliefs are said to be "mythical ideas," which means that they are:
a. almost completely unreal.
b. perfect representations of reality.
c. symbolic postures that reflect partly what is ideal and partly what is real.
d. perverted images of reality, as in the case of totalitarianism.

6. Political conflict within a nation is produced by the following two social conditions:
a. geographical size and racial diversity.
b. scarcity and opposing values.
c. militant culture and class stratification.
d. scarcity and ethnic diversity.

7. When compared with citizens in European democracies, Americans:
a. emphasize self-reliance and trust in the marketplace for security.
b. feel that success in life is determined by forces outside their control.
c. are willing to use government for redistributing economic resources.
d. a and b only.
e. a, b and c.

8. The American ideal of equality of opportunity has been difficult to attain for all except which of the following groups of citizens:
a. African Americans.
b. Americans of Chinese descent.
c. Native American Indians.
d. men of European background.
e. women

9. The relatively low levels of spending on social welfare in the United States most clearly reflects the American ideal of:
a. unity.
b. self-government.
c. equality.
d. individualism.
e. simplicity.

10. A major characteristic of American politics is pluralism, which is:
a. the power to make authoritative and binding decisions.
b. belief in equal distribution of economic resources.
c. competition for power among a great many interests of all kinds.
d. limiting access to power in society to a select few citizens.

11. When people are able to control policy decisions and prevail in political conflicts they are said to have:
a. political power.
b. political authority.
c. pluralism.
d. individualism.
e. diversity.

12. Fragmentation of authority in American politics is illustrated by its:
a. pervasive welfare system.
b. system of checks and balances.
c. economic complexity.
d. geographical diversity.
e. belief in "one person, one vote."

13. The American commitment to the principle of constitutionalism means that:
a. there is tyranny of the majority over the minority.
b. there are limits to the rightful power of government over citizens.
c. direct democracy will be favored over representative democracy.
d. a "mixed economy" must be upheld at all costs.

14. The two kinds of inputs in the political system are termed:
a. laws and decisions.
b. supports and demands.
c. branches of government.
d. culture and socialization.

15. When socialist and capitalist elements of economics are combined it is called:
a. pure free-enterprise capitalism.
b. communism.
c. a fixed economy.
d. a mixed economy.
e. impossible to mix the two.

Essays

1. Explain the meaning of the ideals of equality, diversity, liberty and individualism. Next, discuss how the American political experience contains a conflict between equality and diversity on the one hand and liberty and individualism on the other. Support your essay with examples of these ideals as well as areas where the conflict emerges.

2. Explain the three rules of the game (democratic procedures, constitutionalism and capitalism) that affect the operations of American politics. How do these rules affect the benefits that accrue to participants? How are they applied differently in other countries?

3. Identify and explain the core principles associated with majoritarianism, pluralism and elitism. Which of these theories of power seems to describe the realities of the workings of American politics? Why or why not?

4. Politics in the United States is distinguished from that of other countries by major patterns that include, for instance, a highly fragmented governing system and an extraordinary emphasis on individual rights. Discuss some other major identifying patterns, explaining each briefly and offering some contrasts with other nations.

ANSWER KEY

True/False

1. F	5. T	9. F
2. T	6. F	10. F
3. T	7. F	
4. T	8. F	

Multiple Choice

1. c	6. b	11. a
2. d	7. a	12. b
3. b	8. d	13. b
4. e	9. d	14. b
5. c	10. c	15. d

CHAPTER TWO
- CONSTITUTIONAL DEMOCRACY -

LEARNING OBJECTIVES

After reading this chapter students should be able to

1. Explain the importance of self-government and limited government to Americans.
2. Compare the concepts of "separation of power" and "separated institutions sharing power" as limits on concentration of power.
3. Describe the significance of the Declaration of Independence.
4. Explain the major differences between the Virginia and New Jersey plans.
5. Differentiate between the Federalist and Antifederalist positions on ratification of the Constitution.
6. Define the purpose for a constitution.
7. Describe the checks and balances on the powers of the three branches of American government.
8. Explain the significance of the *Marbury* v. *Madison* law case and the concept of judicial review.
9. Discuss the difference between the use of the terms "republic" and "democracy" by the Framers of the U.S. Constitution.
10. Summarize the arguments for and against direct democratic government, as compared to an indirect, representative government.
11. Contrast between presidential and parliamentary systems of government.

FOCUS AND MAIN POINTS

This chapter describes how the principles of self- and limited government are embodied in the Constitution and explains the tension between them. The chapter also indicates how these principles have been modified in practice in the course of American history, then closes with a brief analysis of the contemporary situation. The main points that are discussed in the chapter are:

- America during the colonial period developed traditions of limited government and self-government.

- The Constitution provides for limited government mainly by defining lawful powers and by dividing those powers among competing institutions.

- The Constitution in its original form provided for self-government mainly through indirect systems of popular election of representatives.

- The idea of popular government--in which the majority's desires have a more direct and immediate impact on governing officials--has gained strength since the nation's beginning.

CHAPTER SUMMARY

The Constitution of the United States is a reflection of the colonial and revolutionary experiences of the early Americans. Freedom from abusive government was a reason for the colonies' revolt against British rule, but the English tradition also provided ideas about government, power, and freedom that were expressed in the Constitution and, earlier, in the Declaration of Independence.

The Constitution was designed to provide for a limited government in which political power would be confined to its proper uses. Liberty has been a basic value of America's political tradition and was a reason for the colonies' revolt against British rule. The Framers wanted to ensure that the government they were creating would not itself be a threat to freedom. To this end, they confined the national government to expressly granted powers and also denied it certain specific powers. Other prohibitions on government were later added to the Constitution in the form of stated guarantees of individual liberties--the Bill of Rights. The most significant constitutional provision for limited government, however, was the separation of powers among the three branches. Powers given to each branch enable it to act as a check on the exercise of power by the others, an arrangement which, during the nation's history, has in fact served as a barrier to abuses of power.

The Constitution, however, did not describe how the powers and limits of government were to be judged in practice. In its historic ruling in *Marbury* v. *Madison,* the Supreme Court assumed the authority to review the constitutionality of legislative and executive actions and to declare them unconstitutional and thus invalid.

The Framers of the Constitution respected the idea of self-government but distrusted popular majorities. They designed a government that they felt would temper popular opinion and slow its momentum, so that the public's "true interest" (which includes a regard for the rights and interests of the minority) would guide public policy. Different methods were established to select members of the House of

Representatives and of the Senate, the president, and federal judges as a means of separating political power from momentary and unreflective majorities.

Since the adoption of the Constitution, however, the public has gradually assumed more direct control of its representatives, particularly through measures affecting the ways in which officeholders are chosen. Political parties, presidential voting (linked to the Electoral College), direct election of senators, and primary elections are among the devices aimed at strengthening the majority's influence. These developments are rooted in the idea, deeply held by ordinary Americans, that the people must have substantial direct control of their government if it is to serve their real interests.

MAJOR CONCEPTS

Antifederalists--the label given to the opponents of the ratification of the Constitution.

Bill of Rights--the first ten amendments to the Constitution.

checks and balances--the elaborate system of divided spheres of authority provided by the U.S. Constitution as a means of controlling the power of government. Separation of powers among the branches of the national government, federalism, and the different methods of selecting national officers are all part of this system.

constitution--provides for limited government by defining lawful powers including the principles according to which a country is organized.

constitutional democracy--a government that is democratic in its provisions for majority influence through elections and is constitutional in its provisions for minority rights and rule by law.

delegates--the idea of elected representatives as being obligated to carry out the expressed wishes of the electorate.

democracy--a form of government in which the people govern, either directly or through elected representatives.

denials of power--a constitutional means of limiting governmental action by listing those powers that government is expressly prohibited from using.

Electoral College--provided that the president would be selected by electors chosen by the states.

electoral votes--assigned to states based upon the total number of members of Congress assigned to the states.

Federalists--those who supported the ratification of the Constitution.

grants of power--the method of limiting the U.S. government by confining its scope of authority to those powers expressly granted in the Constitution.

Great Compromise--provided for a bicameral (two-chamber) Congress: the House of Representatives would be apportioned among the states on the basis of population and the Senate on the basis of an equal number of votes (two) for each state.

inalienable (natural) rights--those rights which persons theoretically possessed in the state of nature, prior to formation of governments. These rights, including those of life, liberty and property, are considered inherent and as such are inalienable. Since government is established by people, government has the responsibility to preserve these rights.

judicial review--the power of courts to decide whether a governmental official or institution has acted within the limits of the Constitution and, if not, to declare its action null and void.

limited government--a government that is subject to strict limits on its lawful uses of powers and hence on its ability to deprive people of their liberty.

New Jersey (small-state) Plan--called for a stronger national government with power to tax and regulate commerce among the states.

primary elections--election to nominate candidates for office in which the rank-and-file voters are given the opportunity to select party nominees.

representative democracy--a system in which the people participate in the decision-making process of government not directly but indirectly, through the election of officials to represent their interests.

republic--historically, the form of government in which representative officials met to decide on policy issues. These representatives were expected to serve the public interest but were not subject to the people's immediate control. Today, the term *republic* is used interchangeably with *democracy.*

self-government--the principle that the people are the ultimate source and proper beneficiary of governing authority; in practice, a government based on majority rule.

separated institutions sharing power--the principle that as a way to limit government, its powers should be divided among separate branches, each of which also shares in the power of the others as a means of checking and balancing them. The result is that no one branch can exercise power decisively without the support or acquiescence of the others.

separation of powers--a way to check power with power by dividing the authority of government so that no single institution could exercise great power without the agreement of other institutions.

trustees--the idea that elected representatives are obligated to act in accordance with their own consciences concerning which policies are in the best interests of the public.

tyranny of the majority--the potential of a majority to monopolize power for its own gain to the detriment of minority rights and interests.

Virginia (large-state) Plan--provided that the states would have numerical representation in Congress in proportion to their populations or tax contributions.

BOXES, TABLES AND FIGURES IN THE TEXT

Boxes
> Limits on Government in the U.S. Constitution
> How the U.S. Compares: Checks and Balances (U.S. and other
> > democracies)
> States in the Nation: Direct Democracy: The Initiative and Referendum

Tables
> Goals of Framers of the Constitution
> Methods of Choosing National Leaders

Figures
    African-Americans as Percentage of State Population
    The System of Checks and Balances

INTERNET RESOURCES

Information about political behavior in general and how democracy works in other countries can be found at: http://www.ghar.dtu.dk/~itsjg/macpherson.html.

More detailed information about the meaning of the word "democracy" and "republic" can be found at: http://www.primenet.com/%7Econduit/.

Positions of the Federalists and Anti-federalists can be found at: http://vi.uh.edu/pages/alhmat/ratdeb.html.

To find the Declaration of Independence from the Library of Congress document collection try: http://lcweb.loc.gov/exhibits/declara/declara4.html.

This site provides an in-depth look at the history of the Declaration of Independence: http://www.nara.gov/exhall/charters/declaration/decmain.html

A 1764-1789 timeline of events leading up to, during, and following the Revolutionary War can be found at: http://memory.locgov/ammen/bdsds/timeline.html

A site that focuses on Andrew Jackson and his role in shaping U.S. politics can be located at: http://odur.let.rug.nl/~usa/P/aj7/about/bio/jackxx.htm

A source that includes documents on the roots of the Constitution, the American Revolution, and the Constitutional Convention is: http://www.yale.edu/lawweb/avalon/constpap.htm

The papers of Thomas Jefferson including his autobiography can be found at: http://www.yale.edu/lawweb/avalon/presiden/jeffpap.htm

ANALYTICAL THINKING EXERCISES

A. Turn to the Constitution in the text. Searching through the Constitution, find at least one example appropriate to each of the twelve categories listed below. Refer to them by their Article or Amendment and their Section. For instance, the clause establishing qualifications for Senators appears in Article I, Section 3. If you are unable to locate an example of one of the categories, formulate a reason why the powers for such a category might be entirely absent from the Constitution. The categories are:

1. Explicit grant of power to:
   a. the states--
   b. the President--
   c. the Congress--
   d. the courts--
2. Implicit grant of power to:
   a. the states--
   b. the President--
   c. the Congress--
   d. the courts--
3. Explicit denial of power to:
   a. the states--
   b. the President--
   c. the Congress--
   d. the courts--

B. Turn to "The Mischiefs of Faction" by James Madison at the end of Chapter Two. Apply the analytical thinking criteria in Chapter One of this *Study Guide* to describing and discussing the content of this reading.

TEST QUESTIONS FOR REVIEW

True/False

1. John Locke maintained that a government, if originally put into place by legitimate means, could never be revoked legitimately.

2. The case of *Marbury* v. *Madison* established the power of the Supreme Court to decide the constitutionality of an act of Congress.

3. In a parliamentary democracy, policy is made by direct referendum from the people since there is no legislature.

4. There is no provision in the U.S. Constitution for any form of direct popular participation in public policymaking, such as a national referendum.

5. The staggered terms of office for the House, Senate and president were devised by the writers of the Constitution in order to provide voters with more frequent opportunities to go to the polls.

6. The U.S. Constitution was an attempt to strike a balance between between representative government and limited government.

7. Over time the American national political system has become more responsive to popular majorities.

8. Federal justices are the only national leaders who can serve for life unless they are impeached or have committed a crime.

9. Since presidential electors have been chosen on the basis of popular vote, there has not been a president elected who lost the popular vote and won the electoral vote.

10. Thomas Jefferson's "Revolution of 1800" was based on rejection of the elite-centered politics of President John Adams.

Multiple Choice

1. Locke's conception of inalienable rights and the legitimacy of the social contract found its most explicit statement in:
a. original state constitutions.
b. the Constitution of the United States.
c. the Declaration of Independence.
d. colonial charters.

2. The principle of checks and balances is based on the notion that:
a. leaders are the trustees of the people.
b. a weak government is always preferable to a strong government.
c. all legislative and executive action should be controlled through judicial power.
d. power must be used to offset power.

3. In *Federalist* No.10, Madison warns against the dangers of:
a. judicial review.
b. factions.
c. allowing *habeas corpus*.
d. an independent executive.

4. As part of its power to "check" the courts, Congress has the constitutional authority to:
a. decide the number of Supreme Court justices.
b. decide the appellate jurisdiction of the Supreme Court.
c. impeach and remove federal judges.
d. a and b only.
e. a, b and c.

5. In practice, the most significant restraint imposed by Congress on the president is its:
a. ability to override presidential vetoes.
b. power of impeachment.
c. power to make the laws and appropriate money.
d. power to approve presidential appointees.

6. Which goals did the writers of the U.S. Constitution seek for government?
1. imperialism
2. self-government
3. limited government
4. anarchy
a. 1 and 2.   b. 2 and 4.   c. 1 and 3.   d. 2 and 3.   e. 3 and 4.

7. Judged in the context of U.S. history, the most effective constitutional constraint on abuses of power is:
a. the separation of powers.
b. judicial review.
c. denials of power.
d. grants of power.

8. The traditional objection to democratic government is the risk of:
a. tyranny of the majority.
b. elite rule.
c. special-interest politics.
d. a weak presidency.

9. Under which principle are minority rights and interests protected by putting restraints on the majority:
a. separation of powers.
b. self-government.
c. checks and balances.
d. judicial review.

10. Formation of the "grass-roots" political party meant that:
a. the era of environmental protection had begun.
b. party politics would no longer be dominated by New Englanders.
c. party politics would be based on participation at the local level by ordinary citizens.
d. party elites would finally be able to dominate nominations for public office.

11. All of the following reforms were accomplished during the Progressive era except:
a. direct election of senators.
b. the initiative and referendum.
c. direct election of the president.
d. primary elections.

12. Charles Beard's thesis about American government is that:
a. democracy should not have been established in such a large country.
b. the poor and uneducated were bound to destroy popular sovereignty.
c. there is no way that a nation can prevent tyranny of the majority.
d. the Constitution was written to keep power in the hands of an elite.

13. In arguing that representatives should use their own judgment in deciding how best to serve their constituencies, Edmund Burke supported the view of representatives as:
a. delegates.
b. trustees.
c. sovereigns.
d. electors.

14. Under the U.S. government under the Articles of Confederation:
a. the states were supreme in power over the national government.
b. the states were subordinate to the national government in all ways.
c. sovereignty was placed in the hands of France.
d. New York was forbidden to enter into trade with New Hampshire.

15. The effectiveness of separation of powers in the United States government is illustrated in your text by:
a. the ability to keep the government from expanding its powers.
b. the Watergate affair in the Nixon administration.
c. America's inability to respond to external aggression quickly.
d. the evolution of judicial review.

16. The "Great Compromise" called for a Congress based on:
a. equal representation for the states.
b. equal representation in one house and population-based representation in the other house.
c. representation based on tax contributions.
d. representation based on a "three fifths" racial formula.

17. Shay's Rebellion drew attention to:
a. the weakness of the national government under the Articles of Confederation.
b. the opposition of the smaller states to the Virginia Plan.
c. Antifederalists' opposition to ratification of the Constitution.
d. states' rights advocates and their fears of a domineering national government.

Essays

1. The U.S. Constitution provides for separated political institutions in the legislature, executive and judicial branches. Explain how each of these branches can check the powers of the others while at the same time having to share some powers with the other branches.

2. Discuss three of the key ideas found in Madson's *Federalist* No. 10.

3. Explain how the system of government of the United States is more democratic in some ways that those of other democracies, yet in other ways is less directly responsive to numerical majorities.

4. Name the four goals of the writers of the Constitution mentioning some ways that their goals relate to applying the Constitution to current issues.

ANSWER KEY

True/False

1. F	5. F	9. F
2. T	6. T	10. T
3. T	7. T	
4. T	8. T	

Multiple Choice

1. c	6. d	11. c	16. b
2. d	7. a	12. d	17. a
3. b	8. a	13. b	
4. e	9. b	14. a	
5. c	10. c	15. b	

CHAPTER THREE
- FEDERALISM -

LEARNING OBJECTIVES

After reading this chapter students should be able to:

1. Define federalism and distinguish among federalist, unitary and confederation governing structures.
2. Differentiate among enumerated, implied and reserved powers in the U.S. Constitution.
3. Describe the evolution of interpretations of the "necessary and proper," "supremacy" and "commerce" clauses of the Constitution.
4. Identify the various states' rights positions.
5. Distinguish between dual and cooperative federalism.
6. Distinguish between federal grants-in-aid, categorical grants and block grants.

FOCUS AND MAIN POINTS

The main focus of this chapter is on the development and evolution of federalism. It reviews the constitutional debate in 1787 over the relationship between the nation and the states describing how the issue of federalism helped shape the Constitution. The chapter's concluding sections discuss how federalism has changed during the nation's history with an overview of contemporary federalism. The chapter's main points are:

- The power of government must be equal to its responsibilities. The Constitution was needed because the nation's preceding system (under the Articles of Confederation) was too weak to accomplish its expected goals, particularly those of a strong defense and an integrated economy.

- Federalism--the Constitution's division of governing authority between two levels, nation and states--was the result of political bargaining.

- Federalism is not a fixed principle for allocating power between the national and state governments, but a principle that has changed over the course of time in response to changing political needs.

- Contemporary American federalism tilts toward national authority, reflecting the increased interdependence of American society. However, there is a current trend toward reducing the scope of federal authority.

CHAPTER SUMMARY

Perhaps the foremost characteristic of the American political system is its division of authority between a national government and the states. The first U.S. government, established by the Articles of Confederation, was essentially a union of states.

In establishing the basis for a stronger national government, the U.S. Constitution also made provisions for safeguarding state interests. The result was the creation of a federal system in which sovereignty was vested in both national and state governments. The Constitution enumerates the general powers of the national government and grants it implied powers through the "necessary and proper" clause. Other powers are reserved to the states by the Tenth Amendment.

From 1789 to 1865, the nation's survival was at issue. The states found it convenient at times to argue that their sovereignty took precedence over national authority. In the end, it took the Civil War to cement the idea that the United States was a union of people, not of states. From 1865 to 1937, federalism reflected the doctrine that certain policy areas were the exclusive responsibility of the national government, while others belonged exclusively to the states. This constitutional position permitted the laissez-faire doctrine that big business was largely beyond governmental control. It also allowed the states in their public policies to discriminate against African Americans. Federalism in a form recognizable today began to emerge in the late 1930s.

In the areas of commerce, taxation, spending, civil rights and civil liberties, among others, the federal government now has an important role, one that is the inevitable consequence of the increasing complexity of American society and the interdependence of its people. National, state and local officials now work closely together to solve the country's problems, a situation that is described as cooperative federalism. Grants-in-aid from Washington to the states and localities have been the chief instrument of national influence. States and localities have received billions in federal assistance; in accepting that money, they have also accepted both federal restrictions on its use and the national policy priorities that underlie the granting of the money.

In recent years, the relationship between the nation and the states has again become a priority issue. Power is shifting downward to the states, and a new balance in the ever-evolving system of U.S. federalism is taking place. This change, as has been true throughout U.S. history, has sprung from the demands of the American people.

MAJOR CONCEPTS

block grants--federal grants-in-aid that permit state and local officials to decide how the money will be spent within a general area, such as education or health.

categorical grants--federal grants-in-aid to states and localities that can be used only for designated projects.

commerce clause--the clause of the Constitution (Article I, section 8) that empowers the federal government to regulate commerce among the states and with other nations.

confederacy--a governmental system in which sovereignty is vested entirely in subnational (state) governments.

cooperative federalism--the situation in which the national, state and local levels work together to solve problems.

devolution--the passing down of authority from the national government to states and localities.

dual federalism--a doctrine based on the idea that a precise separation of national power and state power is both possible and desirable.

enumerated powers (expressed powers)--the seventeen powers granted to the national government under Article I, section 8 of the Constitution. These powers include taxation and the regulation of commerce as well as the authority to provide for the national defense.

federalism (federal system)--a governmental system in which authority is divided between two sovereign levels of government: national and regional.

fiscal federalism--the expenditure of federal funds on programs run in part through state and local governments.

grants-in-aid--cash payments from the federal government to states and localities for programs which they administer.

implied powers--the federal government's constitutional authority (through the "necessary and proper" clause) to take action that is not expressly authorized by the Constitution but which supports actions that are so authorized.

"necessary and proper" clause (elastic clause)--the authority granted to Congress in Article I, section 8 of the Constitution "to make all laws which shall be necessary and proper" for the implementation of its enumerated powers.

reserved powers--the powers granted to the states under the Tenth Amendment to the Constitution.

sovereignty--the ultimate authority to govern within a certain geographical area.

supremacy clause--Article VI of the Constitution, which makes national law supreme over state law when the national government is acting within its constitutional limits.

unitary system--a governmental system in which the national government alone has sovereign (ultimate) authority.

BOXES, TABLES AND FIGURES IN THE TEXT

Boxes
> How the United States Compares: Federal versus Unitary Governments
> States in the Nation: Federal Grants-in-Aid as a Percent of Total State Revenue

Figures
> Federalism as a Governing System: Examples of National, State, and Concurrent Powers
> Federal and State/Local Government Employees, as a Percent of Total Government Employees Who Work in Selected Policy Areas
> Federal, State, and Local Shares of Government Revenue
> Federal Grants to State and Local Governments in Constant (1987) Dollars, 1955-2000

INSTRUCTIONS FOR READING CHARTS, GRAPHS AND FIGURES

Chapter Three contains a different looking map (p. 90) from Chapter One and a pie chart (Figure 3-3, p. 86) and line graph (Figure 3-4, p. 88) which were not included in Chapter One. The instructions that follow should help you interpret them.

1. Find the titles for Figures 3-1, 3-2, 3-3 and 3-4 following the instructions given in Chapter One. For example, the title for Figure 3-4 is "Federal Grants to State and Local Governments in Constant (1987) Dollars, 1955-2000.

2. Next, look at the numbers on the graph for Figure 3-4 to find out what they represent. The clues for telling you this are at the top of the figure and along the left side or across the bottom of it. The vertical axis (on the left side going up) for Figure 3-4 tells you how many billions of dollars (in 1987 dollars) were received in federal grants to state and local governments. The horizontal axis (across the bottom) tells you in what fiscal years the grants were received.

    The pie chart on page 86 differentiates the information about state and local governments from that of the federal government by using different shades of gray. The shading in Figure 3-3 in itself does not add any more information but does dramatize the differences in federal aid to states more than a single line would have shown.

    The map in the box "States in the Nation" uses shading to present differences in the percent of state revenue supplied by federal grants-in-aid. The key for what the color of shading indicates is on the graph.

3. The point that Figure 3-4 makes is underneath the title. It tells you that federal aid to states and localities has increased dramatically since the 1950s. The point Figure 3-3 makes is to show that the federal government raises more revenue than all state and local governments combined.

4. The information presented in Figure 3-4 makes the reader aware that federal grants to states have risen from 1955 to 2000 because the graph gets taller as one reads from left to right, with the tallest peak on the right in 1997 falling in between the lines of 160-180 billions of dollars.

5. The source for information in Figure 3-3 is the U.S. Department of Commerce. Find the source for Figure 3-4.

INTERNET RESOURCES

A source for comparing world constitutions is:
    http://www.uni-hamburg.de/law/index.html.

State government information is available through the National Association of State Information Resource Executives at:
    http://www.state.ky.us/nasire/NASIREhome.html.

The Council for State governments can be reached at:
    http://www.statesnews.org

More about federalism can be found at:
    http://www.urban.org/PERIODCL/pubsect/derthick.htm.

A site containing congressional documents and debates from 1774-1873 can be found at: http://lcweb2.loc.gov/ammem/amlaw/lawhome.html

The site of the Center for the Study of Federalism located at Temple University offers information and publications on the federal system. It can be located at: http://www.temple.edu/federalism

A documentary record of the Federalist Papers, the Annapolis Convention, the Articles of Confederation, the Madison Debates, and the U.S. Constitution can be located at: http://www.yale/edu/lawweb/avalon/federal/fed.htm

ANALYTICAL THINKING EXERCISES

1. Using Table 3-2, answer the following questions:

    A. Name the policy area in which the highest percent of federal government employees are working.
    B. Name the policy area in which the highest percent of state and local level employees are working.
    C. Based on this table, what general conclusion would you draw about the dominance of state and local governments in key policy areas?

2. Read the essay by Samuel H. Beer, "The National Idea in American Politics" at the end of Chapter Three and apply the analytical thinking criteria mentioned in Chapter One of this *Study Guide* to it.

TEST QUESTIONS FOR REVIEW

True/False

1. Federalism is the name given to a way to allocate power between the nation and the states.

2. The supremacy clause protects state power in providing that state law is supreme to conflicting national law.

3. The authority of the national government is specified by the Constitution's enumerated and implied powers. Authority not granted in this way is left to the states as reserved powers.

4. In the *McCulloch* case, the meaning of the "necessary and proper" clause was tested over the issue of whether the national government could establish a postal service.

5. In 1886, the Supreme Court ruled that corporations were "persons" under the Fourteenth Amendment and thus could protect their property rights from state regulation.

6. In the twentieth century, the national government expanded its economic power, supported by its superior taxing powers and a broad interpretaton of the commerce clause.

7. Block grants allow state and local officials to exercise discretion in the national government over the use of federal funds within broad categories such as education or health.

8. Under the first national government based on the Articles of Confederation, the American national government was weak because the central government had no way short of war on states to make them comply with laws.

9. In terms of constant dollars (dollars adjusted for the rate of inflation), federal grants-in-aid have increased tenfold in the past four decades.

10. Most countries in the world have a federalist type government similar to that of the United States.

Multiple Choice

1. The writers of the Constitution established a federal system of government because:
a. the states already existed as sovereign entities.
b. it was consistent with the philosophy expressed in the Declaration of Independence.
c. Locke and Montesquieu concluded it was superior to other systems of government.
d. the British political system was based on the federal principle.

2. Modern day federalism requires the recognition of which of the two following countervailing trends:
a. partial contraction of national authority.
b. increased intrusion of the courts in the national economy.
c. long-term expansion of national authority.
d. a and c only.
e. a and b only.

3. Which one of the following was not one of the results of the Republican Revolution of 1995:
a. reducing unfunded mandates.
b. eliminating the all grant programs to states.
c. decentralized federalism.
d. enacting the Welfare Reform Act a year later.

4. The Constitution allows the states to:
a. raise an army in peacetime.
b. print money.
c. make commercial agreements with other states without the consent of Congress.
d. govern intrastate commerce.

5. The purpose of the Tenth Amendment was to:
a. make sure that the doctrine of national supremacy was absolute.
b. protect the states against national encroachment.
c. end slavery by the year 1808.
d. assign specific delegated powers to the states.

6. In *McCulloch* v. *Maryland*, the Supreme Court ruled:
a. for states' rights.
b. that the "necessary and proper" clause was a restriction on the power of Congress.
c. that the supremacy clause did not prohibit states from taxing the national bank.
d. in favor of national authority.

7. The doctrine of "dual federalism" maintains that:
a. the national government and the states had authority over strictly defined and mutually exclusive domains of policy.
b. any law passed by the national government was the supreme law of the land.
c. the national government and the states should share authority equally in all policy areas.
d. conflicts between the authority of the national government and the states should be resolved by direct appeal to the people.

8. From the 1860s through the mid-1930s, the Supreme Court's rulings on the commerce clause tended to:
a. uphold and expand the Fourteenth Amendment.
b. expand the authority of the national government over the states.
c. strike down national laws aimed at big business, but strongly support state attempts to regulate commerce and labor practices.
d. vigorously support big business at the expense of both national and state authority.

9. National authority has greatly expanded in the twentieth century primarily because:
a. the states and their citizens have become increasingly interdependent.
b. constitutional amendments have opened the way for wider application of national authority.
c. state governments have shown themselves to be an ineffective level of government.
d. Democrats have been in control of Congress for most of the century.

10. Fiscal federalism refers to:
a. the coordinated fiscal policy decisions of the federal government and the states.
b. expenditure of federal funds on programs run in part through state and local governments.
c. distribution of tax revenues between the federal government and the states.
d. the fact that both the federal government and the states have the power to tax.

11. Major types of federal government assistance to states today include:
a. categorical grants.
b. block grants.
c. New Federalism grants.
d. a and b only.
e. a, b and c.

12. Which one of the following is not a theory concerning the relationship between the power and authority of the states and the federal government:
a. pluralism.
b. states' rights.
c. dual federalism.
d. cooperative federalism.
e. New Federalism.

13. Specific powers assigned to Congress by the Constitution are called:
a. implied powers.
b. derived powers.
c. inherent powers.
d. enumerated powers.
e. reserved powers.

14. The term devolution is used to explain:
a. the current trend to shift authority from the federal government
    to state and local governments.
b. the necessity for keeping federal and state spheres of responsibility
    absolutely separate from each other.
c. a failed political revolution.
d. increased recognition that the industrial economy is not confined by
    state boundaries and must be subject to some level of national
    regulation.

15. A government is sovereign when it:
a. loses its identity to another political unit.
b. possesses ultimate governing authority over a certain geographical area.
c. collects revenues in excess of its expenses.
d. has the support of a majority of its citizens.
e.   must defer to a decision from a more powerful political unit.

Essays

1. Identify several problems relating to the Articles of Confederation that led to the proposal to draft a new U.S. Constitution. How did the Constitution address these problems?

2. Explain the differences among dual federalism, states' rights, cooperative federalism and the new federalism of the Reagan era, concluding with a current day appraisal of federalism.

3. Explain what the implied powers doctrine is and how it has been interpreted to strengthen the powers of the national government.

4. Explain what the term "devolution" means when used to describe relationships between states and the federal government and discuss several programs that have been enacted under this approach. What is your assessment of public support for devolution?

ANSWER KEY

True/False

1. T	5. T	9. T
2. F	6. T	10. F
3. T	7. T	
4. F	8. T	

Multiple Choice

1. a	6. d	11. d
2. d	7. a	12. a
3. b	8. d	13. d
4. d	9. a	14. a
5. b	10. b	15. b

CHAPTER FOUR
- CIVIL LIBERTIES -

LEARNING OBJECTIVES

After reading this chapter students should be able to:

1. Define and give examples of some civil liberties.
2. Explain what freedom of expression means.
3. Identify and explain Supreme Court guidelines for free speech.
4. Identify and explain Supreme Court guidelines for free press.
5. Explain the incorporation process for rights of free expression.
6. Explain the differences between establishment and free exercise of religion.
7. Identify what the right of privacy is and what it protects.
8. Explain the differences between procedural and substantive due process.
9. Explain how the process of selective incorporation has been used for procedural rights.
10. Summarize current public attitudes about crime.

FOCUS AND MAIN POINTS

This chapter addresses the topic of civil liberties which are specific individual rights that are constitutionally protected against infringement by government.
These liberties include freedom of speech, press, religion and privacy. An important challenge for civil society is to establish a proper balance between the need for public safety and the practice of individual freedom. Current developments in civil liberties include expansion of individual rights at the same time when society is demanding enhanced protection of collective interests. The main points covered in this chapter are the following:

- Freedom of expression is the most basic of democratic rights, but, like all rights, it is not unlimited. Individual rights are constantly being weighed against the demands of majorities and the collective needs of society.

- "Due process of law" refers to legal protections (primarily procedural safeguards) designed to ensure that individual rights are respected by government.

- During the last half century, the civil liberties of individual Americans have been substantially broadened in law and given greater judicial protection from action by all levels of government. Of special significance has been the Supreme Court's use of the Fourteenth Amendment to protect these individual rights from action by state and local governments.

CHAPTER SUMMARY

In their search for personal liberty, Americans added the Bill of Rights to the Constitution shortly after its ratification. These amendments guarantee certain political, procedural and property rights against infringement by the national government. Freedom of expression is the most basic of democratic rights. People are not free unless they can freely express their views. Nevertheless, free expression may conflict with the nation's security needs during times of war and insurrection. The courts at times have allowed government to limit expression substantially for purposes of national security. In recent decades, however, the courts have protected a very wide range of free expression in the areas of speech, press, and religion.

The guarantees embodied in the Bill of Rights originally applied only to the national government. Under the principle of selective incorporation of these guarantees into the Fourteenth Amendment, the courts extended them to state governments, though the process was slow and uneven. In the 1920s and 1930s, First Amendment guarantees of freedom of expression were given protection from infringement by the states. The states, however, continued to have wide discretion in criminal proceedings until the early 1960s, when most of the fair-trial rights in the Bill of Rights were given federal protection.

"Due process of law" refers to legal protections that have been established to preserve individual rights. The most significant form of these protections consists of procedures or methods (for example, the right of an accused person to have an attorney present during police interrogation) designed to ensure that an individual's rights are upheld. A major controversy in this area is the breadth of the exclusionary rule, which bars the use in trials of illegally obtained evidence. The right of privacy, particularly as it applies to the abortion issue, is also a source of controversy.

Civil liberties are not absolute but must be balanced against other considerations (such as national security or public safety) and against one another when different rights come into conflict. The judicial branch of government, particularly the Supreme Court, has taken on much of the responsibility for protecting and interpreting individual rights. The Court's positions have changed with time and conditions, but the Court has generally been more protective of and sensitive to civil liberties than have elected officials or popular majorities.

MAJOR CONCEPTS

Bill of Rights--the first ten amendments to the Constitution which set forth basic protections for individual rights to free expression, fair trial and property.

civil liberties--the fundamental individual rights of a free society, such as freedom of speech and the right to a jury trial, which in the United States are protected by the Bill of Rights.

clear-and-present-danger test--a test devised by the Supreme Court in 1919 in order to define the limits of free speech in the context of national security. According to the text, government cannot abridge political expression unless it presents a clear and present danger to the nation's security.

due-process clause--a clause in the Fourteenth Amendment which refers to the legal procedures that have been established as a means of protecting individuals' rights.

establishment clause--the First Amendment provision that government may not favor one religion over another, or religion over no religion, and that prohibits Congress from passing laws respecting the establishment of religion.

exclusionary rule--the legal principle that government is prohibited from using in trials evidence that was obtained by unconstitutional means (for example, illegal search and seizure).

free-exercise clause--a First Amendment provision that prohibits the government from interfering with the practice of religion or from prohibiting the free exercise of religion.

freedom of expression--Americans' freedom to communicate their views, the foundation of which is the First Amendment rights of freedom of conscience, speech, press, assembly and petition.

imminent-lawless-action test--limits the authority of a state to restrict speech that advocates the unlawful use of force unless that speech is likely to produce such action.

libel--a written offense that greatly harms a person's reputation.

prior restraint--government prohibition of speech or publication before the fact, which is presumed by the courts to be unconstitutional unless the justification for it is overwhelming.

procedural due process--the constitutional requirement that government must follow proper legal procedures before a person can be legitimately punished for an alleged offense.

selective incorporation--the absorption of certain provisions of the Bill of Rights (for example, freedom of speech) into the Fourteenth Amendment so that these rights are protected from infringement by the states.

slander--a spoken offense that greatly harms a person's reputation.

symbolic speech--conduct that is designed to express an opinion.

BOXES, TABLES AND FIGURES IN THE TEXT

Boxes
> States in the Nation: The Death Penalty
> How the U.S. Compares: Law and Order

Tables
> Selective Incorporation of Rights of Free Expression
> Selective Incorporation of Rights of the Accused

INTERNET RESOURCES

General resources on law and related legal topics can be found through the Washington University Gopher Server. Through Telnet access ACC.WUACC.EDU. After the login request type: WASHLAW.

Supreme Court opinions can be located by using the Federal Court Locator at http://www.law.vill.edu/Fed-Ct/fedcourt.html. Supreme Court decisions can be located through the Cornell Law Library at: http://www.law.cornell.edu/supct/supct.table.html.

Information on Supreme Court rulings especially for nineteenth-century cases can be found at: http://oyez.nwu.edu/index.html

The American Civil Liberties Union site provides information on current civil liberties and civil rights issues, including information on recent and pending Supreme Court cases: http://www.aclu.org/

An excellent source of information on Supreme Court and lower court rulings can be found at: http://www.findlaw.com/casecode/sureme.html

A site dedicated to criminal justice questions with links to many additional sites that focus on particular issues can be reached at: http://www.stpt.usf.edu/~greek/cj.html

ANALYTICAL THINKING EXERCISE

Apply the analytical thinking guidelines from Chapter One of this *Study Guide* to the chapter reading on "The Internet and Free Expression: *Reno v ACLU* law case.

TEST QUESTIONS FOR REVIEW

True/False

1. Although the Constitution says that Congress shall pass "no law" restricting freedom of speech, the Supreme Court's interpretation of the Constitution has specified instances in which congressional limitation of speech is lawful.

2. Prior restraint refers to the Fourth Amendment's prohibition on unreasonable search and seizure by law enforcement officials.

3. The clear-and-present-danger test was developed by the Supreme Court in response to the Sedition Act of 1798.

4. Selective incorporation is the process by which the Fourteenth Amendment has been interpreted to protect liberties listed in the Bill of Rights from infringement by the states.

5. When the two conflict, the First Amendment's free exercise clause takes precedence over the establishment clause.

6. The exclusionary rule holds that evidence obtained through unlawful search and seizure is inadmissible in court.

7. The Supreme Court has tended to be more protective of and sensitive to civil liberties than have elected officials or popular majorities.

8. The Supreme Court ruling in the *Roe* v. *Wade* abortion case derived from an earlier ruling upholding the right of privacy.

9. Since the 1980s, Supreme Court decisions have tended to weaken the protections of the exclusionary rule for defendants.

10. Amnesty International found that the United States ranks lowest in the number of people it places behind bars and in the length of sentences for various categories of crime.

Multiple Choice

1. One constitutional freedom not found in the First Amendment is the right to:
a. peaceable assembly.
b. free exercise of religion.
c. petition the government.
d. fair trial.

2. The individual freedoms in the Bill of Rights were extended by the Fourteenth Amendment to include:
a. the right to privacy.
b. the right to libel public officials.
c. actions of the federal government.
d. actions of state and local governments.

3. In the twentieth century, the limitations of freedom of political expression have been defined primarily in terms of:
a. economics.
b. religion.
c. national security.
   d. public morality.

4. "Justice" in the U.S. criminal justice system is defined primarily in terms of whether:
a. the proper procedures for conviction have been followed.
b. those convicted have the opportunity for appeal.
c. those convicted are actually guilty.
d. those convicted are treated humanely while imprisoned.

5. The doctrine of "prior restraint" is most closely associated with issues of:
a. religious tolerance.
b. freedom of press.
c. artistic expression.
d. sexual mores.

6. Publication of information known to be false and harmful to a reputation is termed:
a. libel.
b. slander.
c. sensationalism.
d. prior restraint.

7. The legal interpretation of "obscenity" is based on:
a. contemporary community standards, regardless of those of any single community.
b. general, social standards regardless of those of any single community.
c. both community and societal standards.
d. common law precedent.

8. A federal law requiring prayer in public schools would be struck down under the:
a. free-exercise clause.
b. establishment clause.
c. exclusionary rule.
d. clear-and-present-danger test.

9. All except for which one of the following is considered to be a right of procedural due process?
a. the prohibition of unlawful search and seizure.
b. the right to have an attorney.
c. the protection against self-incrimination.
d. the right to assembly.

10. The right of privacy is:
a. guaranteed as a specific protection in the Bill of Rights.
b. established by constitutional amendment after the Bill of Rights.
c. inferred from the content and spirit of rights formally declared in the Bill of Rights.
d. used to incorporate certain Bill of Rights freedoms under the Fourteenth Amendment.

11. Free expression can be denied to individuals if it:
a. endangers national security.
b. wrongly damages the reputations of others.
c. is found offensive or disagreeable by society.
d. a and b only.
e. a, b and c.

12. All of the following are individual protections under the concept of procedural due process except for which one:
a. the right to have legal counsel cannot be denied by the states.
b. protection from self-incrimination when testifying.
c. protection from unreasonable search and seizure.
d. protection from prior restraint.

13. Which one of the following is not a "test" applied by the Supreme Court to determine whether government action is lawful:
a. whether general rules are applied fairly to all groups.
b. application of different rules for groups depending upon whether the public likes or dislikes particular groups.
c. right to privacy.
d. imminent lawless action.

14. The term that refers primarily to procedures that authorities must follow before a person can legitimately be punished for an offense is:
a. the three-point test.
b. the right to privacy.
c. procedural due process.
d. substantive due process.
e. suspension of the writ of *habeas corpus*.

15. The Supreme Court decision in *Miranda* v. *Arizona* provided that:
a. police inform suspects of their right to reasonable search and seizure.
b. courts provide indigent defendants with a lawyer.
c. police inform suspects of their rights at the time of arrest.
d. the death penalty for felony offenses violated Eighth Amendment protections against "cruel and unusual punishment."

Essays

1. Describe briefly the difference between the religious guarantees of free exercise and establishment of religion. What guidelines has the Supreme Court established to protect Americans from an establishment of religion. Be sure to include the three-point test.

2. More and more Americans seem willing to go along with diminishing procedural protections for the accused. Given recent Supreme Court guidelines in this area, do you think that America is treating people as if they are guilty until proved innocent instead of the other way around?

3. Your text suggests that the test of a truly civil society is not its treatment of popular ideas and of its best citizens but its willingness to tolerate ideas that the majority detests and to respect equally the rights of its least popular citizens. Do you agree with this point of view? Why or why not?

4. New frontiers requiring guidelines for free speech are the internet and cable television channels. Do you find the content of material to be problematic? What do you think the Supreme Court ought to do in confronting this area of expression? Why?

ANSWER KEY

True/False

1. T	5. F	9. T
2. F	6. T	10. F
3. F	7. T	
4. T	8. T	

Multiple Choice

1. d	6. a	11. d
2. d	7. c	12. d
3. c	8. b	13. c
4. a	9. d	14. c
5. b	10. c	15. c

CHAPTER FIVE
- EQUAL RIGHTS -

LEARNING OBJECTIVES

After reading this chapter students should be able to:

1. Distinguish between civil liberties and civil rights.
2. Explain what "equality under the law" means.
3. Explain the significance of the *Brown* v. *Board of Education* decision.
4. Discuss the problems women face today in overcoming discrimination.
5. Highlight efforts to overcome discrimination towards Native Americans, Hispanic Americans and Asian Americans.
6. Describe the differences among the reasonable-basis test, the strict-scrutiny test and suspect classifications.
7. Discuss the provisions of the Civil Rights Act of 1964.
8. Distinguish between *de jure* and *de facto* segregation.
9. Explain what affirmative action was designed to achieve.

FOCUS AND MAIN POINTS

This chapter focuses on equal rights, or civil rights, which are terms referring to the right of every person to equal protection under the law and equal access to society's opportunities and public facilities. Equal rights emphasizes whether individual members of different groups--racial, sexual, and others--are treated equally by government and, in some areas, by private parties. The history of civil rights has been largely one of group claims to equality. Civil liberties deal with issues of personal freedom, and civil rights involve issues of equality.
The chapter emphasizes the following main points:

- Disadvantaged groups have had to struggle for equal rights.

- Americans have attained substantial equality under the law. They have, in legal terms, equal protection of the laws, equal access to accommodations and housing, and an equal right to vote.

- Legal equality for all Americans has not resulted in *de facto* equality.

- African Americans, women, Hispanic Americans, and other traditionally disadvantaged groups are given a disproportionately small share of America's opportunities and benefits.

CHAPTER SUMMARY

During the past few decades, the United States has undergone a revolution in the legal status of its traditionally disadvantaged groups, including African Americans, women, Native Americans, Hispanic Americans, and Asian Americans. Such groups are now provided equal protection under the law in areas such as education, employment and voting. Discrimination by race, sex and ethnicity has not been eliminated from American life but is no longer substantially backed by the force of law.

Traditionally disadvantaged Americans have achieved fuller equality primarily as a result of their struggle for greater rights. The Supreme Court has been an important instrument of change for minority groups. Its ruling in *Brown v. Board of Education* (1954), which declared racial segregation in public schools to be an unconstitutional violation of the Fourteenth Amendment's equal-protection clause, was a major breakthrough in equal rights. Through its busing, affirmative action and other rulings, the Court has also mandated the active promotion of integration and equal opportunities.

However, because civil rights policy involves large issues of social values and the distribution of society's resources, questions of civil rights are politically explosive. For this reason, legislatures and executives as well as the courts have been deeply involved in such issues, siding at times with established groups and sometimes backing the claims of underprivileged groups. Thus Congress, with the support of President Lyndon Johnson, enacted the landmark Civil Rights Act of 1964; but Congress and recent presidents have been ambivalent about or hostile to busing for the purpose of integrating public schools.

In recent years affirmative action programs, designed to achieve equality of result for African Americans, women, Hispanic Americans and other disadvantaged groups, have been a civil rights battleground. Affirmative Action has had the strong support of civil rights groups and has won the qualified endorsement of the Supreme Court, but has been opposed by those who claim that it unfairly discriminates against white males. Busing is another issue that has provoked deep divisions within American society.

MAJOR CONCEPTS

affirmative action-- a term that refers to programs designed to ensure that women, minorities and other traditionally disadvantaged groups have full and equal opportunities in employment, education and other areas of life.

comparable worth--the idea that women should get pay equal to men for work that is of similar difficulty and responsibility and that requires similar levels of education and training.

de facto discrimination--discrimination on the basis of race, sex, religion, ethnicity and the like that results from social, economic and cultural biases and conditions.

de jure discrimination--discrimination on the basis of race, sex, religion, ethnicity, and the like that results from a law.

equal-protection clause--a clause of the Fourteenth Amendment that forbids any state to deny equal protection of the laws to any individual within its jurisdiction.

equal rights (civil rights)--the right of every person to equal protection under the laws and equal access to society's opportunities and public facilities.

equality of result--the objective of policies intended to reduce or eliminate the effects of discrimination so that members of traditionally disadvantaged groups will have the same benefits of society as do members of advantaged groups.

gender gap--the tendency of women to vote more heavily Democratic than men do.

intermediate-scrutiny test--a test applied by courts to laws that treat individuals unequally. Such a law may be deemed constitutional if it serves a clearly compelling and justified purpose.

reasonable-basis test--a test applied by courts to laws that treat individuals unequally. Such a law may be deemed constitutional if its purpose is held to be "reasonably" related to a legitimate government interest.

strict-scrutiny test--a test applied by courts to laws that attempt a racial or ethnic classification. In effect, the strict-scrutiny test eliminates race or ethnicity as a legal classification when it places minority group members at a disadvantage.

<u>suspect classifications</u>--legal classifications, such as race and national origin, that have invidious discrimination as their purpose and are therefore unconstitutional.

BOXES, TABLES AND FIGURES IN THE TEXT

<u>Boxes</u>
> States in the Nation: Black and Latino Representation in State   Legislatures
> How the U.S. Compares: Women's Inequality

<u>Tables</u>
> Hispanics' Party Identification, By National Origin
> Levels of Court Review for Laws That Treat Americans Differently
> Key Decisions in the History of Affirmative Action Policy

<u>Figures</u>
> The Gender Gap in Congressional Voting
> Mortgage Application Rejections
> U.S. Per Capita Income, By Race and Ethnicity
> Increase in De Facto School Segregation

INTERNET RESOURCES

If you have audio capabilities, Supreme Court decisions can be heard orally by first downloading and installing a program called RealAudio that allows you to hear the arguments. RealAudio can be reached on the web at http://www.realaudio.com. For decisions after 1955: http://oyez.at.nwu.edu/oyez.html.

Special information regarding slavery can be found at: http://vi.uh.edu/pages/mintz/primary.htm. Other issues regarding the experience of black people in America can be found at: http://www.gatech.edu/bgsa/blackpages.html.

Information about Dr. Martin Luther King can be found at: http://www.seattletimes.com/mlk/

Information is available regarding other minorities affected by equal rights rulings including Native Americans, Asian Americans, Hispanic Americans, Americans with disabilities, women and issues affecting women. Some examples of sources are:
> National Organization for Women at http://www.now.org/
> Native Americans: http://www.cowboy.net/native/
> Hispanic Americans: http://www.latinoweb.com/favision/resource.htm

Asian Americans: http://asianamculture.miningco.com

The American Indian Research and Policy Institute was established by Native Americans in 1992. Its site includes a political and legal history of Native Americans and examines current issues affecting them. It can be located at: http://www.airpi.org/

A detailed look at the history and culture of African Americans contained in the Library of Congress exhibition entitled *The African American Odyssey: A Quest for Full Citizenship* can be found at: http://lcweb2.loc.gov/ammem/aaohtml

The web site for the National Council of La Raza (NCLR), an organization dedicated to improving the lives of Hispanics, contains information on public policy, immigration, citizenship, and other subjects. It can be found at: http://www.nclr.org

The web site for the Center for the American Woman and Politics (CAWP) at Rutgers University's Eagleton Institute of Politics is dedicated to enhancing women's influence and leadership in public life. It is located at: http://wizard.ucr.edu/~asampaio/cawp.html

ANALYTICAL THINKING EXERCISE

Read and review the reading "America's Racial Divide by William Jefferson Clinton at the end of the chapter. Apply the analytical thinking criteria from Chapter One of this *Study Guide* to the essay.

TEST QUESTIONS FOR REVIEW

True/False

1. The reasonable basis test applies to all laws except those which prescribe differential treatment on the basis of suspect classifications.

2. Passage of the Fourteenth Amendment did not immediately affect the right of private employers to discriminate in their hiring practices.

3. All forms of discrimination on the basis of gender are unconstitutional.

4. Since passage of the Civil Rights Act of 1968, segregation of neighborhood housing has all but disappeared in the United States.

5. In the *Bakke* case, the Supreme Court did not invalidate affirmative action.

6. In terms of incomes, jobs and similar economic indicators, the gap between African Americans and white Americans has diminished steadily since the 1960s.

7. Affirmative Action is intended to help achieve equality of result for African Americans, women, Hispanic Americans, and other disadvantaged groups.

8. The Simpson-Mizzoli Act took citizenship away from legal aliens who had lived continuously in the U.S. for five years.

9. Civil rights and civil liberties mean the same thing regarding legal protection.

10. The Voting Rights Act of 1965 as amended and extended, was declared unconstitutional by the Supreme Court.

Multiple Choice

1. When a law discriminates along racial lines and thus becomes a suspect classification, its constitutionality is subject to the Supreme Court's:
a. strict-scrutiny test.
b. reasonable-basis test.
c. intermediate test.
d. three-pronged test.

2. Disadvantaged Americans have gained their rights:
a. through the enlightened policies of advantaged Americans.
b. through judicial action only.
c. through struggle against entrenched interests.
d. mainly through action by states rather than the federal government.

3. "Redlining" refers to:
a. discrimination by banks in the granting of mortgages and loans.
b. the refusal by hotels to supply service to African Americans.
c. restrictive clauses prohibiting the resale of property to "undesirable" groups.
d. overt discrimination by landlords in their advertisements.

4. Regarding the rights and status of women:
1. the Equal Rights Amendment became the 27th Amendment when it was ratified in 1982.
2. the women's rights movement began in the World War I era and ended with passage of the 19th Amendment.
3. women have made clear gains in the areas of appointive and elective offices.
4. on the average, full-time women employees earn only about three-fourths as much as full-time men employees.
a. 2 and 3.   b. 1 and 4.   c. 1 and 2.   d. 3 and 4.   e. all the above.

5. Asian Americans:
a. make up the only minority group that has not experienced discrimination in America.
b. were at one time denied entry into the United States on account of their race.
c. are over-represented in top positions in society.
d. have been excluded from the 1964 Civil Rights Act.

6. The Supreme Court rejected the constitutionality of "separate but equal" facilities in:
a. *Brown* v. *Board of Education of Topeka.*
b. *Reed* v. *Reed.*
c. *Swann* v. *Charlotte-Mecklenburg County Board of Education.*
d. *Plessy* v. *Ferguson.*

7. In *U.S.* v. *Virginia* the Supreme Court held that:
a. the male-only admission policy at state-supported VMI was unconstitutional.
b. male-only registration for the military draft is constitutional.
c. state-supported male-only colleges are constitutional.
d. women-only colleges are permissible under law.

8. Affirmative action arose as a policy when:
a. it became apparent that disadvantaged Americans would not attain equal employment opportunities through law suits that benefited single individuals only.
b. the Supreme Court declared in *Bakke* that the Fourteenth Amendment requires government and large firms to hire more women and minorities.
c. the Supreme Court ruled that *de facto* discrimination is unlawful.
d. private firms decided on their own that a more diverse workforce was actually a more productive and effective workforce.

9. An example of a policy that aimed chiefly to overcome *de facto* discrimination is:
a. the Equal Rights Amendment.
b. the Voting Rights Act of 1965.
c. busing to achieve racial integration in the schools.
d. "redlining."

10. The Civil Rights Act of 1964 dealt chiefly with discrimination in:
a. schools.
b. housing.
c. public accommodations.
d. voting.

11. Racism in America:
a. ended with the defeat of the South in the Civil War.
b. is a proper issue to address under the concept of civil rights.
c. cannot be addressed under the U. S. Constitution.
d. only pertains to African Americans.

12. Creation of election districts that favor election of minority-group members to Congress:
a. is strictly prohibited by the Voting Rights Act and its extensions.
b. has been encouraged by recent Supreme Court decisions.
c. makes it illegal to redraw election district boundaries to reduce the voting power of a minority group.
d. provides that race cannot be the dominant or deciding factor in redrawing districts especially in Texas, Georgia and North Carolina.

13. The legal standard for sexual harassment in the workplace is:
a. to view women as sex objects in a discrete manner.
b. permit the display of sex-related pictures or objects as long
as women are not forced to view them.
c. to apply the "reasonable woman" standard.
d. to provide separate work areas for men and women within reason.

14. Which of the following statements is not true about the current status of
Native Americans:
a. About half of them live on reservations set aside for them by the
federal government.
b. They are significantly more likely to attend college than other
Americans.
c. They have lower life expectancies than the national average.
d. They have a much higher infant mortality rate than that of white
Americans.

15. Opponents of affirmative action have argued that the policy:
a. results in widespread reverse discrimination against white males.
b. inevitably degenerates into a quota system, and therefore violates the
law.
c. is fair only when it is "victim specific," applying only to those
individuals who are personally discriminated against and hence
deserve to benefit from government intervention.
d. a and c only.
e. a, b and c.

Essays

1. In order to achieve equality of opportunity among all people, does everyone have to be given identical opportunities to succeed? Discuss in the context of information provided in your text.

2. Present the arguments for and against affirmative action. Where do you stand on the issue? Why?

3. Write about at least two disadvantaged groups covered in this chapter, noting their status under the law and gains that have been made. What issues still need to be addressed in order to improve the status of those groups?

4. What are the tests that the Supreme Court uses to decide cases of discrimination under the equal protection clause of the Fourteenth Amendment?

ANSWER KEY

True/False

1. F	3. F	5. T	7. T	9. F
2. T	4. F	6. F	8. F	10. F

Multiple Choice

1. a	5. b	9. c	13. c
2. c	6. a	10. c	14. b
3. a	7. a	11. b	15. e
4. d	8. a	12. d	

CHAPTER SIX
- PUBLIC OPINION AND POLITICAL SOCIALIZATION -

LEARNING OBJECTIVES

After reading this chapter students should be able to:

1. Identify the major factors that influence formation of public opinion.
2. Describe the different survey methods used to measure public opinion.
3. Identify the agents of political socialization and describe their impact.
4. Differentiate between cultural and ideological thinking.
5. Identify what partisan thinking is and what influences it.
6. Describe the influence of public opinion on American policymakers.
7. Identify the essential differences between a liberal and a conservative.

FOCUS AND MAIN POINTS

This chapter discusses public opinion and its influence on the U.S. political system. A major theme is that public opinion is a powerful and yet inexact force in American politics. The policies of the U.S. government cannot be understood apart from public opinion; at the same time, public opinion is not a precise determinant of public policy. The main points made in this chapter are the following:

- Public opinion consists of those views held by ordinary citizens that are publicly expressed.

- The process by which individuals acquire their political opinions is called political socialization. This process begins during childhood and continues into adulthood.

- Americans' political opinions are shaped by several frames of reference, the most important of which are political culture, ideology, group attachments and partisanship.

- Public opinion has an important influence on government but works primarily to channel and impose limits on the choices made by officials.

CHAPTER SUMMARY

Public opinion can be defined as those opinions held by ordinary citizens which government takes into account in making its decisions. Public officials have many ways of assessing public opinion, such as the outcomes of elections, but have increasingly come to rely on public opinion polls. There are many possible sources of error in polls, and surveys sometimes present a misleading image of the public's views. However, a properly conducted poll can provide an accurate indication of what the public is thinking and can dissuade political leaders from thinking that the views of the most vocal citizens (such as demonstrators and letter writers) are also the views of the broader public.

The process by which individuals acquire their political opinions is called political socialization. During childhood the family and schools are important sources of basic political attitudes, such as beliefs about the parties and the nature of the U.S. political and economic systems. Many of the basic orientations that Americans acquire during childhood remain with them in adulthood, but socialization is a continuing process. Major shifts in opinion during adulthood are usually the consequence of changing political conditions; for example, the Great Depression of the 1930s was a catalyst for wholesale changes in Americans' opinions on the government's economic role. There are also short-term fluctuations in opinion that result from new political issues, problems and events. Individuals' opinions in these cases are affected by prior beliefs, peers, political leaders and the news media. Events themselves are also a significant short-term influence on opinions.

The frames of reference that guide Americans' opinions include cultural beliefs, such as individualism, which result in a range of acceptable and unacceptable policy alternatives. Opinions can also stem from ideology, although most citizens do not have a strong and consistent ideological attachment. In addition, individuals develop opinions as a result of group orientations, notably religion, income, occupation, region, race, gender or age. Partisanship is perhaps the major source of political opinions; Republicans and Democrats differ in their voting behavior and views on many policy issues. However, party loyalty has declined in importance in recent decades as a frame of reference for people's opinions.

Public opinion has a significant influence on government but seldom determines exactly what government will do in a particular instance. Public opinion constrains the policy choices of officials. Some policy actions are beyond the range of possibility because the public will not accept change in existing policy or will not seriously consider policy that seems clearly at odds with basic American values. Evidence indicates that officials are reasonably attentive to public opinion on highly visible and controversial issues of public policy.

MAJOR CONCEPTS

<u>Age-cohort tendency</u>--holds that a significant break in the pattern of political socialization is almost always concentrated among younger citizens.

<u>agents of socialization</u>--influences on socialization such as family, schools, peers, the mass media, and political leaders and events.

<u>conservatives</u>--those who emphasize the marketplace as the means of distributing economic benefits but look to government to uphold traditional social values.

<u>ideology</u>--a consistent pattern of opinion on political issues that stems from a basic underlying belief or set of beliefs.

<u>liberals</u>--those who favor activist government as an instrument of economic security and equitable redistribution of resources but reject the notion that government should favor a particular set of social values.

<u>libertarians</u>--those who oppose government as an instrument of traditional values and of economic security.

<u>party identification</u>--the personal sense of loyalty that an individual may feel toward a particular political party.

<u>political socialization</u>--the learning process by which people acquire their political opinions, beliefs and values.

<u>population</u>--in a public opinion poll, the term *population* refers to the people (for example, the citizens of a nation) whose opinions are being estimated through interviews with a sample of those people.

<u>populists</u>--those who favor activist government as a means of promoting both economic security and traditional values.

<u>primacy tendency</u>--refers to the fact that what is learned first is often lodged most firmly in one's mind.

<u>probability sample</u>--a sample for a poll in which each individual in the population has a known probability of being selected randomly for inclusion in the sample.

<u>public opinion</u>--those opinions held by ordinary citizens that they express openly.

<u>public opinion poll</u>--a device for measuring public opinion whereby a relatively small number of individuals (the sample) are interviewed for the purpose of estimating the opinions of a whole community (the population).

sample--in a public opinion poll, the relatively small number of individuals who are interviewed for the purpose of estimating the opinions of an entire population.

sampling error--a measure of the accuracy of a public opinion poll. The sampling error is mainly a function of sample size and is usually expressed in percentage terms.

structuring tendency--refers to the tendency of earlier learning to structure later learning.

BOXES, TABLES AND FIGURES IN THE TEXT

Boxes
      How the U.S. Compares: Citizens' Awareness of Public Affairs
      States in the Nation: Conservatives and Liberals
Tables
      Approximate Sampling Error by Number of Opinion-Poll Respondents
Figures
      Public Opinion on Taxing and Spending
      Relationship Between Sample Size and Sampling Error
      Opinions on Religion
      Types of Ideologies
      Gender and Opinion
      Partisanship and Issue Opinions
      Partisan Identification

INTERNET RESOURCES

Some general web sources for public opinion research and polling include:

      National Opinion Research Center: http://www.norc.uchicago.edu/
      Pew Research Center: http://www.people-press.org/
      Gallup Polling Group: http://www.gallup.com.

A site that provides nonpartisan information about current public issues is: http://www.policy.com/

The Princeton Survey Research Center's site offers results from surveys conducted by a variety of polling organizations at: http://www.princeton.edu;80/~abelson/index.html
The nonpartisan Public Agenda's site provides opinions, analyses, and educational materials on current policy issues at: http://www.publicagenda.org/

For information about some ideological groups:

Communitarians: http://www.gwu.edu/~ccps/
Libertarians: http://www.libertarian.com/wwlp
Left-wing: http://www.tiac.net/users/rafeb/
Right-wing: http://www.clark.net/pub/jeffd/index.html

ANALYTICAL THINKING EXERCISES

A. Note in the chapter the identifying characteristics of liberals and conservatives. Go back through previous chapters and add other identifying qualities to that list. Look at all the items on the list and then notice where they are logically consistent and where they are not. Note which items might actually conflict with each other within each list. See if there are any items on the list that seem to characterize your beliefs. Consider how actual individual opinions falling into more ambiguous areas than the traditional liberal-conservative typology.

B. Apply the analytical thinking criteria to the essay "Democracy, Information, and the Rational Public" by Benjamin Page and Robert Shapiro at the end of Chapter Six in your text.

TEST QUESTIONS FOR REVIEW

True/False

1. Rather than having one stable, uniform public opinion that public policy makers can tap for reinforcement, America is described as a nation of many publics.

2. The larger the sample, the smaller the sampling error.

3. Political socialization refers only to the learning that takes place during childhood years.

4. More women favor strict gun control laws than men.

5. "Party identification" refers to a person's vote, Republican or Democrat, in the most recent election.

6. Scholars have concluded that only a minority of citizens readily understand and apply an ideological frame of reference to political issues.

7. In a democracy, elections are the only reliable indicator of public opinion on issues.

8. A person who professes beliefs in economic individualism and traditional social values is known as a conservative.

9. Party loyalties can be altered by changes in social and economic conditions.

10. Public opinion in America tends to constrain rather than direct the policy choices of officials.

Multiple Choice

1. The process by which individuals acquire their political opinions is most accurately known as:
a. popular conditioning.
b. social communication.
c. socio-economic propaganda.
d. political socialization.

2. Which of the following poll results are theoretically the most accurate, assuming that all have a confidence level of .95:
a. sample size = 2,000; population size - 250 million.
b. sample size = 1,000; population size - 100,000.
c. sample size = 1,500; population size - 35 million.
d. sample size = 500; population size - 25,000.

3. In their study of public opinion and policy, Benjamin Page and Robert Shapiro concluded that:
a. there is no relationship between public opinion and public policy.
b. when public opinion changes, public policy then follows in the same direction.
c. when public policy changes, public opinion then follows in the same direction.
d. policy change tends to follow opinion change, but only on less important issues.

4. In general, public opinion:
a. determines government action.
b. is unrelated to government action.
c. sets broad limits on government action.
d. affects government action only on issues that are prominent in elections.

5. During a period of dealignment:
a. the outcome of elections is extremely predictable.
b. a new dominant party arises.
c. voter turnout and enthusiasm increase.
d. instability develops within existing party coalitions.

6. Since 1960, Americans have increasingly considering themselves to be:
a. liberals.
b. independents.
c. Republicans.
d. Democrats.

7. The chief agents for political socialization include all except which one of the following:
a. family.
b. peers.
c. education.
d. corporations.

8. Frames of reference that guide American political thinking include:
1. political cultural thinking.
2. ideological thinking.
3. group attachments.
4. partisan identification.
a. 3 and 4.   b. 1, 3, 4.   c. 1 and 3.   d. 2, 3, 4.   e. all the above.

9. Partisan thinking is linked to:
a. loyalty to a political party.
b. preference for interest groups over political parties.
c. voting for the individual rather than the party.
d. considering oneself an independent.

10. Liberalism and conservatism are given in the text as examples of:
a. political parties.
b. partisan thinking.
c. cultural idealism.
d. ideologies.

11. Indicators of public opinion in the United States include all except which one of the following:
a. election results.
b. size of crowds at demonstrations.
c. number of newspapers sold.
d. letters to editors of newspapers.

12. Major characteristics mentioned in the text to describe the process of political socialization include:
1. what is learned first is often lodged most firmly in one's mind.
2. socialization continues throughout life.
3. early learning structures what is learned later.
4. an extraordinary event can alter beliefs especially for younger adults.
a. 1 and 3.   b. 2 and 4.   c. 1, 2, 3.   d. 2, 3, 4.   e. all the above.

13. Discovering how Americans think politically can be important in which respects:
a. it can provide clues about how public opinion is likely to affect government.
b. a shared frame of reference can bring citizens together in the pursuit of a common goal.
c. it can reveal how truly alienated public opinion is from the actions of government in a democratic political system.
d. a and b only.
e. a, b and c.

14. The major characteristics of the process of political socialization include all except which one of the following:
a. primacy tendency.
b. structuring tendency.
c. age-cohort tendency.
d. reverse tendency.

15. Public opinion assumes more importance in democratic societies than in non-democratic ones because of the:
a. president's power as commander in chief.
b. availability of polls.
c. legal requirement for a national referendum on presidential war actions.
d. belief that the source of government is the will of the people.
e. need to mobilize the populace to action.

Essays

1. How have family, schools, peers and media influenced your political socialization? Think about people and incidents that have affected your attitude about politics. Explain how it all fits together to create your political framework.

2. If a person used only polling information upon which to make political decisions, what elements of the information should the decision maker take into account? What are some liabilities of relying solely on polling information for major political decisions?

3. Using material provided in the text about the low level of political information possessed by Americans (despite a relatively open and free media network), the relatively unstructured way Americans are socialized about politics and their lack of partisan thinking, how do you account for the survival of democracy in America?

4. Would you consider yourself a liberal, conservative, populist or libertarian? Explain the major defining characteristics of each of these ideologies before applying them to your own belief structure.

ANSWER KEY

True/False

1. T	3. F	5. F	7. F	9. T
2. T	4. T	6. T	8. T	10. T

Multiple Choice

1. d	4. c	7. d	10. d	13. d
2. a	5. d	8. e	11. c	14. d
3. b	6. b	9. a	12. e	15. d

CHAPTER SEVEN
- VOTING AND PARTICIPATION -

LEARNING OBJECTIVES

After reading this chapter students should be able to:

1. Identify the factors that relate to low voter turnout in U.S. elections.
2. Discuss how the U.S. compares with other nations in voter turnout.
3. Distinguish between prospective and retrospective voting.
4. Identify what factors account for differences in voter turnout among groups in American elections.
5. Identify conventional ways of engaging in political activity other than voting.
6. Identify what unconventional political participation is and how it has impacted public policy.
7. Describe how American individualism and class bias affect participation.

FOCUS AND MAIN POINTS

This chapter focuses on political participation in its various forms. It highlights voting as the most common form of political activity, examining factors that affect voter turnout. Citizen participation is an important component of democratic societies and needs to be encouraged. This chapter explains differences in the extent of political participation among various American groups and compares America's participation patterns with citizens in other Western democracies. Major points made in this chapter are the following:

- Voter turnout in U.S. elections is low compared with other democratic nations, which may relate to differences in registration requirements, frequency of elections and the nature of political parties.

- Although most Americans do not participate actively in politics other than by voting, they are more active than citizens of other democracies.

- Most Americans make a sharp distinction between their personal lives and national life, which reduces their incentive to participate politically.

CHAPTER SUMMARY

Political participation is an involvement in activities designed to influence public policy and leadership. A main issue of democratic government is the question of who participates in politics and how fully they participate.

Voting is the most widespread form of active political participation among Americans. Yet voter turnout is significantly lower in the United States than in other democratic nations. The requirement that Americans must personally register in order to establish their eligibility to vote is one reason for lower turnout among Americans; other democracies place the burden of registration on government officials rather than on the individual citizen. The fact that the United States holds frequent elections also discourages some citizens from voting regularly. Finally, the major American political parties, unlike many of those in Europe, do not clearly represent the interests of opposing economic classes; thus the policy stakes in American elections are correspondingly lower. Some Americans do not vote because they think that policy will not change greatly regardless of which party gains power.

Prospective voting is one way that people can exert influence on policy through their participation. It is the most demanding approach to voting: voters must develop their own policy preferences and then educate themselves about the candidates' positions. Most voters are not well-enough informed about the issues to respond in this way. Retrospective voting demands less from voters: they need only decide whether the government has been performing well or poorly in terms of the goals and values they hold. Evidence suggests that the electorate is, in fact, reasonably sensitive to past governmental performance, particularly in relation to economic prosperity.

Only a minority of citizens engage in the more demanding forms of political activity, such as work on community affairs or on behalf of a candidate during a political campaign. The proportion of Americans who engage in these more demanding forms of activity exceeds the proportion of Europeans who do so. Nevertheless, only about one in every four Americans will take an active part in a political organization at some point in their lives. Most political activists are individuals of higher income and education; they have the skills and material resources to participate effectively and tend to take greater interest in politics. More than in any other Western democracy, political participation in the United States is related to economic status.

Social movements are broad efforts to achieve change by citizens who feel that government is not properly responsive to their interests. These efforts sometimes take place outside established channels: demonstrations, picket lines and marches are common means of protest. Protesters are younger and more idealistic on average than other citizens, but they are a very small proportion of the population. In addition, protest activities do not have much public support, despite the country's tradition of free expression.

Overall, Americans are only moderately involved in politics. They are concerned with political affairs, but are mostly immersed in their private pursuits,

71

a reflection in part of our culture's emphasis on individualism. The lower level of participation among low-income citizens has particular significance in that it works to reduce their influence on public policy and leadership.

MAJOR CONCEPTS

alienation--a feeling of personal powerlessness that includes the notion that government does not care about the opinions of people like oneself.

apathy--a feeling of personal non-interest or unconcern with politics.

civic duty--the belief that civic and political participation is a responsibility of citizenship.

political participation--a sharing in activities designed to influence public policy and leadership such as voting, joining political parties and interest groups, writing to elected officials, demonstrating for political causes and giving money to political candidates.

prospective voting--a form of electoral judgment in which voters choose the candidate whose policy promises most closely match their own preferences.

registration--the practice of placing citizens' names on an official list of voters before they are eligible to exercise their right to vote.

retrospective voting--a form of electoral judgment in which voters support the incumbent candidate or party when their policies are judged to have succeeded and oppose the candidate or party when their policies are judged to have failed.

social capital--consists of the sum of the face-to-face civic interactions among citizens in a society.

social (political) movements--active and sustained efforts to achieve social and political change by groups of people who feel that government has not been properly responsive to their concerns.

suffrage--the right to vote.

voter turnout--the proportion of persons of voting age who actually vote in a given election.

BOXES, TABLES AND FIGURES IN THE TEXT

Boxes
  How the U.S. Compares: Voter Turnout
  State-by-State Voter Turnout in Presidential Elections
Tables
  Opinions on Obligations of Citizens
  Opinions On Election Politics
Figures
  Voter Turnout in Presidential Elections, 1960-1996
  Perceived Effect of Electing a Republican or Democratic President
  Voter Turnout and Income
  Americans' Major News Sources

INTERNET RESOURCES

A convenient way to access government and to contact political officials is through:
http://www.politicalindex.com/

Project Vote Smart, founded by Presidents Ford and Carter, provides general information on voting returns and candidates. It can be found through:
http:/www.vote-smart.org/

Information about young voters can be located at: http:/www.rockthevote.org/

The American Voter Coalition is a national nonpartisan organization dedicated to empowering Americans through voter education and registration. It also provides information on how to register to vote at:
http://www.avc.org

The University of Michigan's National Election Studies (NES) site provides survey data on voting, public opinion, and political participation at:
http://www.umich.edu/~nes/

ANALYTICAL THINKING EXERCISES

A. What are the essential obligations of citizenship illustrated in Table 7-1? Which do Americans consider the most important? least important?

B. Apply the analytical thinking format from Chapter One of this *Study Guide* to the essay "America's Declining Social Capital" by Robert D. Putnam at the end of Chapter Seven in your text.

TEST QUESTIONS FOR REVIEW

True/False

1. Low voter turnout is characteristic of democracies that have extended suffrage to virtually all adults.

2. Voting is the way most Americans directly participate in national politics.

3. Although political participation in the U.S. is much higher among higher-income groups than lower-income groups, the U.S. is no different in this respect from other Western democracies.

4. States with lenient registration requirements do not have significantly higher voter turnout than those with stringent requirements.

5. Senior citizens are the age group with the lowest rate of voter turnout.

6. At some point in their lives, a majority of Americans engage in unconventional political activism.

7. Prospective voting entails holding officials responsible for past actions.

8. The American ideal of individualism promotes a sharp distinction in people's minds between their personal lives and national life.

9. The historical trend in voting qualifications in the U.S. has been to eliminate barriers to political participation.

10. The major source of information for most Americans is television.

Multiple Choice

1. One of the reasons why voter turnout is lower in the United States than in Western European countries is that:
a. Americans pay less attention to politics.
b. U.S. registration laws place a greater burden on the individual.
c. the U.S. population is not as well educated.
d. the U.S. spends less money on the electoral process.

2. Which one of the following would increase voter turnout the most:
a. sharp differences between major political parties.
b. alienation.
c. frequent elections.
d. an individualistic culture

3. The personal characteristic along which participation tends to vary the least is:
a. age.
b. gender.
c. race.
d. socioeconomic class.

4. A knowledge of candidates' issue positions and campaign promises would be most valuable for which type of voting?
a. prospective
b. retrospective
c. split-ticket
d. party line

5. What type of elections tend to draw the largest percentage of voters in the United States?
a. primary
b. mayoral
c. congressional
d. presidential

6. Social movements are a way for:
1. those dissatisfied with government to get its attention.
2. the politically weak to force government to be more responsive to their interests than it normally is.
3. people to present their views through more dramatic means than conventional political activity allows.
4. people to recruit candidates for office.
a. 2 and 4.   b. 2, 3, 4.   c. 1, 2, 3.   d. only 4.   e. all the above.

7. When it comes to protest activities, a majority of Americans are:
a. actively involved at one time or another in their lives.
b. willing to contribute through financial support but not through direct participation in running for office or working for a campaign.
c. not highly supportive of such activities despite America's tradition of free expression.
d. actively involved only at a later stage of their lives when they feel more secure about their positions on issues.

8. All except for which one of the following are conventional forms of political participation in America:
a. voting.
b. campaign activities.
c. participation in social movements.
d. community activities.

9. In 1993 the U.S. motor voter law:
a. required states to register people to vote when they apply for driver's licenses.
b. discouraged people from driving and voting.
c. denied voting to people convicted of drunk driving.
d. denied voting to people on welfare.
e. employed government officials to go from house to house to register people to vote.

10. Which characteristic is most often associated with a frequent voter:
a. low income.
b. youth.
c. apathy.
d. a high level of education.

11. The overall pattern of individual political participation in the U.S.:
a. is almost opposite from the distribution of influence that prevails in the private sector.
b. parallels the distribution of influence that prevails in the private sector.
c. favors poorer citizens.
d. is increased by the American commitment to individualism.

12. When voters hold public officials responsible for past actions at election time, this is called what type of voting?
a. prospective
b. default
c. retrospective
d. mandate

13. Since the 1960s, voter turnout in presidential elections has fallen below _____percent.
a. 20
b. 25
c. 35
d. 40
e. 60

14. The reason the text gives for the 1994 Republican party victories in congressional races is:
a. public disenchantment with Washington politics.
b. severe downturn in the nation's economy.
c. prospective voting.
d. the public's concern for local over national issues.
e. failure of voters to know their incumbent representative's name.

15. Political participation among Americans can best be described as favoring:
a. lower-income groups.
b. females over males.
c. non-white minorities.
d. the middle-class.
e. young over old.

Essays

1. Compare and contrast voting regulations and turnout between the United States and European democracies. Do you think that the United States should take action to improve political participation? Why?

2. Do you think that unconventional political activism is needed in a democratic political system? What purpose does it serve?

3. What factors do you use to assess candidates running for office? Do you depend upon party labels for your initial attraction to a candidate?

4. What role does the media play in voting and participation in American politics? How can its role have a more positive effect on turnout?

ANSWER KEY

True/False

1. F	3. F	5. F	7. F	9. T
2. T	4. F	6. F	8. T	10. T

Multiple Choice

1. b	4. a	7. c	10. d	13. e
2. a	5. d	8. c	11. b	14. a
3. b	6. c	9. a	12. c	15. d

CHAPTER EIGHT
- POLITICAL PARTIES, CANDIDATES AND CAMPAIGNS -

LEARNING OBJECTIVES

After reading this chapter students should be able to:

1. Trace the evolution of the American two-party system.
2. Distinguish between realigning and critical elections.
3. Distinguish between party-centered and candidate-centered politics.
4. Relate single-member election districts with plurality elections to the maintenance of the two party system in America.
5. Describe the distinguishing features of multiparty election systems with proportional representation.
6. Identify several minor parties and describe their role in American politics.
7. Describe what primary elections are and explain their role in American politics.
8. Identify the factors associated with organizational weakness in American parties.
9. Describe the role money plays in modern campaigns.

FOCUS AND MAIN POINTS

This chapter explains that party organizations are alive and well in America but are secondary to candidates as the driving force in contemporary campaigns. It explores the history of U.S. parties, the patterns of party politics and the conduct of modern campaigns. The following points are emphasized in this chapter:

- Political competition in the United States has centered on two parties, a pattern that is explained by the nature of America's electoral system, political institutions and political culture.

- To win an electoral majority, candidates of the two major parties must appeal to a diverse set of interests; this necessity normally leads them to advocate moderate and somewhat overlapping policies.

- U.S. party organizations are decentralized and fragmented. The national organization is a loose collection of state organizations, which in turn are loose associations of autonomous local organizations. The ability of America's party organizations to control nominations and election to office is weak, which in turn enhances the candidates' role.

- Candidate-centered campaigns are based on the media and utilize the skills of professional consultants. Money, strategy, and televised advertising are key components of today's presidential and congressional campaigns.

CHAPTER SUMMARY

Political parties serve to link the public with its elected leaders. In the United States this linkage is provided by a two-party system; only the Republican and Democratic parties have any chance of winning control of government. The reality that the United States has only two major parties is explained by several factors, including an electoral system characterized by single-member districts which makes it difficult for third parties to compete for power. Also, each party accepts a variety of different political views, and the parties exist in a political culture that stresses compromise and negotiation rather than ideological rigidity.

Because the United States has only two major parties, each of which seeks to gain majority support, their candidates normally tend to avoid controversial or extreme political positions. Candidates typically pursue moderate and somewhat overlapping policies. Nonetheless, the Democratic and Republican candidates sometimes do offer sharply contrasting policy alternatives, particularly in times of political unrest.

America's parties are decentralized, fragmented organizations. The national party organization does not control the policies and activities of the state organizations, and they in turn do not control the local organizations. Traditionally the local organizations have controlled most of the party's work force because most elections are contested at the local level. Local parties, however, vary markedly in their vitality. Whatever their level, America's party organizations are relatively weak. They lack control over nominations and elections. Candidates can bypass the party organization and win nomination through primary elections. Individual candidates also control most of the organizational structure and money necessary to win elections. Recently the state and national party organizations have expanded their capacity to provide candidates with modern campaign services. Nevertheless, party organizations at all levels have few ways of controlling the candidates who run under their banner. They assist candidates with campaign technology, workers and funds but cannot compel candidates' loyalty to organizational goals.

American political campaigns, particularly those for higher-level office, are candidate-centered. Most candidates are self-starters who become adept at "the election game." They spend much of their time raising campaign funds and build their personal organizations around "hired guns": pollsters, media producers and election consultants. Strategy and image-making are key components of modern campaigns, as is televised political advertising, which accounts for roughly half of all spending in presidential and congressional races.

Because America's parties cannot control their candidates or coordinate their policies at all levels, they are unable to consistently present voters with a coherent, detailed platform for governing. The national electorate as a whole is thus denied a clear choice among policy alternatives and has difficulty exerting a decisive and predictable influence through elections.

MAJOR CONCEPTS

air wars--applied to candidates' use of televised ads especially by playing off each other's ads, seeking to gain the strategic advantage.

candidate-centered politics--election campaigns and other political processes in which candidates, not political parties, have most of the initiative and influence.

dealignment--a situation in which voters' partisan loyalties have been substantially and permanently weakened.

grassroots party--a political party built from the bottom up consisting of committees and clubs at the local, state, and national levels, with membership open to all eligible voters.

hard money--funding given by a political party and individual contributors to a candidate for office that is regulated by the campaign finance laws and must go directly to the candidate and can be spent as the candidate chooses.

hired guns--modern day campaign organization consisting of consultants, pollsters, media producers, and fund-raising specialists who charge for their services.

money chase--term used to explain the activity of candidates who are forced to spend much of their time raising funds because of the high cost of campaigns.

multiparty system--a system in which three or more political parties have the capacity to gain control of government separately or in coalition.

nomination--the designation of a particular individual to run as a political party's candidate (its "nominee") in the general election.

packaging (of candidates)--the process in a campaign of placing aspects of the candidate's partisanship, policy positions, record, and personality in the context of the voters' "ideal" candidates.

party-centered politics--election campaigns and other political processes in which political parties, not individual candidates, hold most of the initiative and infuence.

party coalition--the groups and interests that support a political party.

party competition--a process whereby conflict over society's goals is transformed by political parties into electoral competition in which the winner gains the power to govern.

party organizations--party organizational units at national, state and local levels; their influence has decreased over time as a result of many factors.

party realignment--an election or set of elections in which the electorate responds strongly to an extraordinarily powerful issue that has disrupted the established political order. A realignment has a lasting impact on public policy, popular support for the parties and the composition of the party coalitions.

political party--an ongoing coalition of interests joined together to get their candidates for public office elected under a common label.

primary election (direct primary)--a form of election in which voters choose a party's nominees for public office. In most primaries, eligibility to vote is limited to voters who are registered members of the party.

proportional representation--a form of representation in which legislative seats are allocated proportionally according to each political party's share of the popular vote. This system enables smaller parties to compete successfully for seats.

service relationship--a situation where party organizations assist candidates for office but have no power to require them to accept or campaign on the party's main policy positions.

single-member districts--a form of representation in which only a single candidate is elected to a particular office by the voters of that district. This system favors major parties because only candidates who can gain a large proportion of votes in an election district have a realistic chance of winning.

soft money--process made possible by a loophole in campaign finance regulation which enables a contributor to give an unlimited amount of money to a political party. This money must be spent only on party activities (rather than the candidate individually) building party membership, getting out the vote through ads and registration drives, and advertising campaigns that raise public awareness about political issues.

split-ticket voting--the pattern of voting in which the individual voter in a given election casts a ballot for one or more candidates of each major party. This pattern is the opposite of straight-ticket voting.

straight-ticket voting--this occurs when a voter in an election casts a ballot that includes only candidates of the same party.

two-party system--a system in which only two political parties have a real chance of acquiring control of the government.

BOXES, TABLES AND FIGURES IN THE TEXT

Boxes
> How the U.S. Compares: Party Systems
> States in the Nation: Party Control of State Legislatures

Tables
> Television Campaign Practices

Figures
> A Graphic History of America's Major Parties
> Vote of Select Demographic Groups in Recent Presidential Election
> Americans' Opinions About the Need for a Strong Third Party
> Organization of the Political Party

INTERNET RESOURCES

Project Vote Smart carries information about campaign finances and a list of U.S. national parties with links to each organization's web page at: http://www.vote-smart.org/organizations/POLITICAL PARTIES/

The Federal Election Commission, including information on PAC money, can be found at: http://www.fec.gov.

For a debate on campaign finance reform go to: http://www.student.mckenna.edu/dduran/cfr.htm

FEC resources about all aspects of elections and campaigns can be found at http://www.fec.gov/index.htm.

Electoral College information and results can be accessed at: http://www.nara.gov/nara/fedreg/ec/

Election tables and graphs from 1952-2000 can be found through American National Election Studies at http://www.umich.edu/~nes/

Sources from *Time and CNN* that cover national politics in general can be found at http://www.allpolitics.com/

The Web offers information on virtually all political parties that run candidates in American elections. Some specific resources are:

Democratic National Committee: http://www.democrats.org/
Republican National Committee: http://www.rnc.org/

Third parties in politics since the 1960s: http://www.greens.org/usa/tphist.html.

Libertarian Party: http://www.lp.org/lp/

Reform Party: http://www.reformparty.org/

For general information about placing candidates or new parties on the ballots in the states, see: http://www.well.com/conf/liberty/ban/

ANALYTICAL THINKING EXERCISES

A. Using Figure 8-2, describe the demographic groups which made up Democratic party support in recent presidential elections. Summarize which groups gave the Democratic party the most support and then figure out which groups then most probably would have supported the Republican party. Decide which party you and your family would most likely match. Which party most nearly matches that of your state and congressional district?

B. Using the analytical thinking format from Chapter One of this *Study Guide,* discuss the reading "Running for Congress" by Paul S. Herrnson at the end of Chapter Eight of your text.

TEST QUESTIONS FOR REVIEW

True/False

1. The two-party system is the most common form of party system in democratic countries.

2. Politics in the U.S. today is best described as party-centered politics.

3. Single member election districts in the U.S. tend to discourage the permanence of minor parties.

4. To be successful, American political parties generally have to adopt moderate positions on issues.

5. U.S. political parties are loose non-hierarchical associations of national, state and local organizations.

6. During a realignment, the party identification of an existing majority of voters changes.

7. Candidate-centered campaigns have increased the accountability of public officials for the actions of government.

8. In the 1930s the Republican party was seen by the electorate as the party of business and wealthy interests.

9. Major American political parties usually take specific positions on controversial issues.

10. The coalitions of voters that make up the Republican and Democratic parties are virtually identical.

Multiple Choice

1. Democrats and Republicans have endured as the two major U.S. parties primarily due to:
a. their ability to adapt to changing circumstances.
b. the stability of their ideologies.
c. the lack of good third-party candidates.
d. a high degree of party discipline.

2. The major structural characteristic that helps perpetuate the American two-party system is:
a. the fact that there are naturally two sides to political disputes.
b. regional conflict.
c. single-member election districts.
d. state laws prohibiting the placement of a third major party on the ballot.

3. The organizational structure of the major U.S. parties can be described as:
a. centralized and fragmented.
b. decentralized and fragmented.
c. decentralized and dependent.
d. centralized and independent.

4. The Prohibition and Right-to-Life parties have been examples of what type of minor political party?
a. single-issue
b. ideological
c. economic
d. factional

5. The greatest blow to the organizational strength of U.S. parties was:
a. the national nominating convention.
b. reforms of Jacksonian democracy.
c. the emergence of PACs.
d. the direct primary election.

6. During the twentieth century, American political parties have lost power over all except which one of the following:
a. nominations for office.
b. financing.
c. public government jobs.
d. get-out-the-vote efforts on election day.

7. The two major U.S. parties tend to build broad coalitions of supporters because of America's tendency toward:
a. moderation.
b. apathy.
c. idealism.
d. tolerance.

8. The "new politics" is characterized by all except which one of the following:
a. television advertising.
b. direct-mail fundraising.
c. door-to-door canvassing.
d. opinion poll analysis.

9. Candidate-centered politics encourages all except which one of the following:
a. greater responsiveness to local interests.
b. flexibility in response to problems.
c. introduction of "new blood" to politics.
d. low-cost campaigns.

10. In a proportional representation party system, seats in a nation's legislature are allocated to the:
a. party with the highest number of people running on the ballot.
b. parties based on the percentage of the popular vote received.
c. winner of a numerical majority who takes all the seats.
d. members of the party who won a plurality of the votes.

11. The primary goal of a major U.S. political party is to:
a. gain control of government by electing its candidates to office.
b. draw attention to a particular issue.
c. increase voter turnout.
d. share in the spoils of office.

12. Rewarding people who worked for party politics by giving them government jobs is called:
a. corruption.
b. party-centered politics.
c. candidate-centered politics.
d. patronage.

13. National and state political parties in modern candidate-centered campaigns:
a. avoid fund raising on behalf of candidates.
b. insist on total control of candidates using the party's label.
c. tend to assume a service role to help candidates get elected.
d. emphasize having a power relationship rather than a service relationship with the candidate.

14. Realigning elections have an important impact on:
a. national policy.
b. party identification.
c. subsequent elections.
d. b and c only.
e. a, b and c.

15. The term "soft money" refers to:
a. use of paper money rather than coins in campaigns.
b. raising money that goes directly to a specific candidate rather than to the party in general.
c. money that is used for media advertising only.
d. money that is given to the political party in general and not specifically targeted for a particular congressional or presidential campaign.

Essays

1. Describe and discuss some major differences in political party organization and function between U.S. and European democracies. Do you think that American politics would function more cohesively with a European style of party operation?

2. Of what use are minor political parties in American politics if they rarely win office and usually do not last as long as the two major parties?

3. Do you think that the trend away from party-centered politics toward candidate-centered politics is healthy for the functioning of America's political system? Are there any aspects of the candidate-centered campaign process you would like to see changed?

4. What are the descriptive characteristics of realigning elections? Do they invigorate political processes or make them more confusing? Do you think that the South is experiencing a realignment?

ANSWER KEY

True/False

1. F	3. T	5. T	7. F	9. F
2. F	4. T	6. F	8. T	10. F

Multiple Choice

1. a	4. a	7. a	10. b	13. c
2. c	5. d	8. c	11. a	14. e
3. b	6. d	9. d	12. d	15. d

CHAPTER NINE
- INTEREST GROUPS -

LEARNING OBJECTIVES

1. Define interest groups and describe what they do.
2. List the different types of interest groups and their constituencies.
3. Distinguish between economic and non-economic interest groups.
4. Distinguish between inside and outside lobbying processes.
5. Identify what functions political action committees fulfill in the political process.
6. Distinguish between iron triangles and issue networks.
7. Explain what grassroots lobbying is.
8. Explain the differences between pluralist theory and "interest group liberalism."
9. Explain the Madisonian dilemma.

FOCUS AND MAIN POINTS

This chapter examines the degree to which various interests in American society are represented by organized groups, the process by which interest groups exert influence and the costs and benefits of group politics regarding the public good. Main points made in the chapter are the following:

- Although nearly all interests in American society are organized to some degree, those associated with economic activity, particularly business enterprises, are by far the most thoroughly organized.

- Lobbying and electioneering are the traditional means by which groups communicate with and influence political leaders.

- When public policy is decided solely by group demands, the group process does not serve the collective interest, regardless of the number of separate interests that benefit from the process.

CHAPTER SUMMARY

A political interest group is a set of individuals organized to promote a shared political concern. Most interest groups owe their existence to factors other than politics. They form for economic reasons, such as the pursuit of profit, and maintain themselves by making profits (in the case of corporations) or by providing their members with private goods such as jobs and wages. Such interest groups include corporations, trade associations, labor unions, farm organizations and professional associations. Collectively, economic groups are by far the largest set of organized interests. The group system tends to favor interests that are already economically and socially advantaged.

Citizens' groups do not have the same organizational advantages as economic groups. They depend on voluntary contributions from potential members who may lack interest and resources, or who recognize that they will get the collective good from a group's activity even if they do not participate (the free-rider problem). These citizens' groups include public interest, single-issue, and ideological groups. Their numbers have increased dramatically since the 1960s despite their organizational problems.

Organized interests seek influence largely by lobbying public officials and contributing to election campaigns. Using an "inside strategy," lobbyists develop direct contacts with legislators, government bureaucrats and members of the judiciary in order to persuade them to accept their group's perspective on policy. Groups also use an "outside strategy," seeking to mobilize public support for their goals. This strategy relies in part on grassroots lobbying--encouraging group members and the public to communicate their policy views to officials.

"Outside" lobbying also includes efforts to elect officeholders who will support group aims. Through political action committees (PACs), organized groups now provide nearly a third of all contributions received by congressional candidates.

The policies that emerge from the group system bring benefits to many interests, and in some instances these benefits also serve the general interest. But when groups can essentially dictate policies, the common good is not served. The majority's interest is subordinated to group (minority) interests.

MAJOR CONCEPTS

citizens' (or non-economic) groups--organized interests formed by individuals drawn together by opportunities to promote a cause in which they believe but which does not provide them significant individual economic benefits.

collective (public) goods--benefits that are offered by groups (usually citizens' groups) as an incentive for membership but that are nondivisible (e.g., a clean environment) and therefore are available to nonmembers as well as members of the particular group.

economic groups--interest groups that are organized primarily for economic reasons but which engage in political activity in order to seek favorable policies from government.

free-rider problem--a situation in which the incentives offered by a group to its members are also available to nonmembers. Incentives to join a group and to promote its cause are reduced because nonmembers (free riders) receive benefits without having to pay any of the group's costs.

grassroots lobbying--a form of lobbying designed to persuade officials that a group's policy position has strong constituent support.

inside lobbying--direct communication between organized interests and policymakers, which is based on the assumed value of close ("inside") contacts with policymakers.

interest group--a set of individuals who are organized to promote a shared political interest.

interest-group liberalism--the tendency of public officials to support the policy demands of self-interested groups (as opposed to judging policy demands according to whether or not they serve a larger conception of "the public interest").

iron triangle--a small and informal but relatively stable group of well-positioned legislators, executives and lobbyists who seek to promote policies beneficial to a particular interest.

issue network--an informal network of public officials and lobbyists who have a common interest and expertise in a given area and who are brought together by a proposed policy in that area.

lobbying--the process by which interest-group members or lobbyists attempt to influence public policy through contacts with public officials.

material incentive--an economic lure such as that for high wages used to attract potential members to join an interest group.

outside lobbying--a form of lobbying in which an interest group seeks to use public pressure as a means of influencing officials.

political action committees (PACs)--organizations through which interest groups raise and distribute funds for election purposes. By law, funds must be raised through voluntary contributions.

private (individual) goods--benefits that a group (most often an economic group) can grant directly and exclusively to individual members of the group.

purposive incentive--reasons for joining a citizens' group. A purposive incentive provides an opportunity to promote a cause in which an individual believes.

single-issue politics--a situation in which separate groups are organized around nearly every conceivable policy issue and press their demands and influence to the utmost.

BOXES, TABLES AND FIGURES IN THE TEXT

Boxes
> How the U.S. Compares: Groups: "A Nation of Joiners"
> States in the Nation: Limits on PAC Contributions in State Elections

Tables
> Advantages and Disadvantages Held By Economic and Citizens' Groups
> Tactics Used In Inside and Outside Lobbying Strategies

Figures
> How an Iron Triangle Benefits Its Participants
> Percentage of PACS by Category

INTERNET RESOURCES

General information on line about interest groups and other volunteer activities can be found at: http://www.impactonline.org/. Most specific interest groups have web pages.

The Federal Election Commission site offers infoirmation on elections, voting, campaign finance, parties and PAC's. Its web address is: http://www.fec.gov/

The Public Interest Research Group site has chapters on many college campuses and provides state-by-state policy and other information. It can be found at: http://www.pirg.org

The web site of the American Conservative Union includes policy and political information as well as a lively chat room. It can be found at: http://www.townhall.com/

The Americans for Democratic Action is a liberal political organization dedicated to individual liberty and building economic and social justice at home and abroad. It can be found at: http://adaction.org

The Sierra Club which promotes conservation and protection of the environment can be visited at: http://sierraclub.org/

To track political action committee money from the Federal Election Commission see: http://www.fec.gov

The Nonprofit Center for Responsive Politics tracks lobbyist and campaign spending. It can be located at: http://www.crp.org

The U.S. Chamber of Commerce can be found at http://www.uschamber.org/

The AFL-CIO web site is: www.aflcio.org/

The American Civil Liberties Union can be located at: http://www.aclu.org

ANALYTICAL THINKING EXERCISES

A. This exercise presents an opportunity to apply some conceptual explanations to commonly found information relating to a topic. Familiarize yourself with the differences between inside and outside lobbying tactics from Table 9-2. From newspapers or newsmagazines find articles describing lobbying activity that illustrates both categories.

B. Apply the anaytical thinking format from Chapter One of this *Study Guide* to the reading "The Paralyzing Effect of Group Politics" by Jonathan Rauch at the end of Chapter Nine of the text.

TEST QUESTIONS FOR REVIEW

True/False

1. A defining characteristic of any interest group is that it exists to promote a single specific policy in a particular political arena.

2. "Pluralists" believe that the actions of interest groups in general have a strongly positive impact on society.

3. Purposive incentives to group membership are based on the opportunity to participate in a cause in which one believes.

4. The free-rider problem presents problems in attracting members to economic interest groups.
5. The dominant interest group for labor is the AFL-CIO.

6. In comparison with citizens' groups, economic groups have an easier time gathering resources necessary for organized political activity.

7. Lobbyists rely primarily on members of Congress who share their views.

8. An issue network is a stable set of bureaucrats, legislators and lobbyists who are concerned with policies beneficial to their common goal.

9. The great bulk of PAC funding is given to incumbents seeking re-election.

10. An interest group seeking favorable coverage by the news media is engaging in outside lobbying.

Multiple Choice

1. The groups that are the most well-financed promote:
a. social services.
b. corporate interests.
c. political ideologies.
d. public interests.

2. James Madison argued:
a. against all interest groups.
b. for regulation of interests through a governing system of checks and balances.
c. for the advocacy of self-interests free from all governmental restraint.
d. for the replacement of interest groups by formal political parties.

3. One of the flaws in pluralist group theory is the fact that:
a. the group system is unrepresentative because some interests are far better organized and more powerful than others.
b. the public interest is never served by policies that promote special interests.
c. larger groups always prevail politically over smaller groups.
d. political parties better represent different interests than do interest groups.

4. The chief way groups lobby the judiciary is through:
a. lobbying justices directly at work.
b. filing lawsuits.
c. influencing the selection of federal judges.
d. a and b only.
e. b and c only.

5. Effective "inside lobbying" is based upon:
a. countering the aims of other groups.
b. mobilizing the group's members.
c. providing useful and persuasive information to key officials.
d. bribing or threatening officials.

6. "Interest group liberalism" refers to:
a. the proliferation of interest groups throughout the Democratic party.
b. the fact that liberal groups are more numerous than conservative ones.
c. the tendency of officials to support the policy demands of the interest group or groups that have a special stake in a policy.
d. the activity of groups in support of liberal causes such as disarmament and environmental protection.

7. The most significant resource that most interest groups can offer congressional candidates is:
a. help with issue research.
b. a promise of campaign volunteers.
c. a promise of votes from members of the group.
d. money.

8. In the working dynamics of an "iron triangle," what benefit do interest groups provide to "friendly" bureaucratic agencies:
a. services for constituents.
b. lobbying support for agency programs.
c. campaign contributions.
d. administration of mutually beneficial policies.

9. The largest number of PACs are those associated with:
a. single-issue groups, such as environmental groups and right-to-life groups.
b. labor.
c. business.
d. agriculture.

10. Interest groups function to:
1. promote public policies.
2. encourage the political participation of their members.
3. support candidates for office.
4. work to influence policymakers.
a. 1 and 3.   b. 1, 2, 3.   c. 2 and 4.   d. 2, 3, 4.   e. all the above.

11. Economic interest groups have an advantage over other groups chiefly because of their:
a. ability to muster large numbers of members.
b. access to financial resources.
c. emphasis on training people to run for Congress.
d. devotion to promoting the free enterprise system.

12. When members of non-economic interest groups promote a cause in which they believe they are pursuing what the text calls:
a. immediate gains.
b. direct economic benefits.
c. selfish interests.
d. purposive incentives.

13. Links between interest groups and the U.S. bureaucracy are most evident in which of the following:
a. the foreign relations committees of Congress.
b. during election years.
c. when a case involving its interests is before the Supreme Court.
d. in the regulatory agencies such as the FCC that oversee the nation's business sectors.

14. Groups such as the Council of State Governments, the National Governors Conference and the U.S. Conference of Mayors illustrate which type of interest group?
a. governments
b. labor
c. economic
d. foreign nations

15. Political Action Committees:
a. raise money for election campaigns by soliciting voluntary contributions from members or employees.
b. can give union dues collected from laborers to candidates running for office.
c. are under no restrictions regarding the amount of money each PAC can give to the election campaign of a single candidate for federal office.
d. are diminishing as an effective influence in political campaigns.

Essays

1. What are the relative advantages and disadvantages held by economic versus citizens' interest groups? Give examples.

2. Discuss what the Madisonian dilemma is and explain whether you think it still applies to today's workings of interest groups.

3. Discuss the advantages and drawbacks of interest group politics toward promoting a democratic system of government. You could include some of the positive and negative aspects of pluralism versus majoritarianism in this essay.

4. Which of the three branches of national government do you think would be hardest to lobby? Explain your choice. (Make sure you mention the basic methods of lobbying each branch in your answer)

ANSWER KEY

True/False

1. F	3. T	5. T	7. T	9. T
2. T	4. F	6. T	8. F	10. T

Multiple/Choice

1. b	4. e	7. d	10. e	13. d
2. b	5. c	8. b	11. b	14. a
3. a	6. c	9. c	12. d	15. a

CHAPTER TEN
- THE NEWS MEDIA -

LEARNING OBJECTIVES

After reading this chapter students should be able to:

1. Identify the stages in the development of America's news media.
2. Describe ways that the government regulates the media.
3. Discuss the factors that encourage uniformity of news coverage by the American media.
4. Define and discuss the four roles of the media.
5. Discuss what is meant by the concept of "partisan neutrality" as applied to the news.

FOCUS AND MAIN POINTS

This chapter focuses on the role of the media in politics. It contends that the news media serves as a different kind of intermediary than either parties or groups and that problems arise when the press is expected to perform the same functions as these institutions. The main ideas presented in this chapter are the following:

- The American press was initially tied to the nation's political party system (the partisan press) but gradually developed an independent position (the objective press).

- Although the United States has thousands of separate news organizations, they present a common version of the news which reflects journalists' shared view of what the news is.

- In fulfilling its responsibility to provide public information, the news media effectively perform three significant roles--those of signaler (the press brings relevant events and problems into public view), common carrier (the press serves as a channel through which political leaders can address the public), and watchdog (the press scrutinizes official behavior for evidence of deceitful, careless or corrupt acts).

- The press cannot do the job of political institutions, even though it increasingly tries to do so.

CHAPTER SUMMARY

In the nation's first century, the press was allied closely with political parties and helped the parties mobilize public opinion. Gradually the press freed itself from this relationship and developed a form of reporting, known as objective journalism, that emphasizes the fair and accurate reporting of newsworthy developments. The foundation of modern American news rests on the presentation and evaluation of significant events, not on the advocacy of partisan ideas. The nation's news organizations do not differ greatly in their reporting; broadcast stations and newspapers throughout the country emphasize many of the same events, issues and personalities, following the lead of the major broadcast networks, a few elite newspapers and the wire services.

The press performs four basic roles in a free society. In their signaler role, journalists communicate information to the public about events and problems that they consider important, relevant, and therefore newsworthy. The press also serves as a common carrier, in that it provides political leaders with a channel for addressing the public. Third, the press acts as a public protector, or watchdog, by exposing deceitful, careless or corrupt officials. The American media can, and to a significant degree does, perform these roles adequately.

The press is less well suited, however, to fulfill the role of public representative. This role requires a consistent political viewpoint and public accountability, neither of which the press possesses. The media cannot be a substitute for effective political institutions. Its strength lies ultimately in its capacity to inform the public, not in its attempts to serve as its representative.

MAJOR CONCEPTS

agenda setting--the power of the media through news coverage to focus the public's attention and concern on particular events, problems, issues, personalities, and so forth.

common-carrier role--the media's function as an open channel through which political leaders can communicate with the public.

descriptive style of reporting--a style of reporting that required that reporters stick to the "facts" which provided a straightforward description of events.

interpretive style of reporting--the style of reporting that aims to explain *why* something is taking place or has occurred.

news--the news media's version of reality, usually with an emphasis on timely, dramatic and compelling events and developments.

objective journalism--a model of news reporting which is based on the communication of "facts" rather than opinions and which is "fair" in that it presents all sides of partisan debate.

partisan press--newspapers and other communication media that openly support a political party and whose news in significant part follows the party line.

press (news media)--those print and broadcast organizations that are in the news-reporting business.

public representative role--a role whereby the media attempt to act as the public's representatives.

signaler role--the accepted responsibility of the media to alert the public to important developments as soon as possible after they happen or are discovered.

watchdog role--the accepted responsibility of the media to protect the public from deceitful, careless, incompetent and corrupt officials by standing ready to expose any official who violates accepted legal, ethical or performance standards.

BOXES, TABLES AND FIGURES IN THE TEXT

<u>Boxes</u>
> States in the Nation: In the News, or Out
> How the U.S. Compares: Partisan Neutrality as a News Value

<u>Figures</u>
> The Public's View of the "New" News
> Negative Coverage of Presidential Candidates, 1960-2000

INTERNET RESOURCES

An excellent source for nonpartisan news and current political issues is:
http://www.politicsusa.com/

More specific media sources include:
ABC - http://www.prognet.com/contentp/abc.html
CBS - http://www.cbs.com/news/
NBC - http://www.msnbc.com/
CNN - http://www.cnn.com/
     http://www.allpolitics.com
PBS - http://www.pbs.org/
USA TODAY - http://www.usatoday.com/

The Center for Media and Public Affairs is a nonpartisan organization that analyzes news coverage on a continuing basis. This web site is useful for anyone interested in the media's political coverage: http://www.cmpa.com

The web site through which Matt Drudge (The Drudge Report has challenged the traditional media's control of the news can be found at: http://www.drudgereport.com

The Federal Communications Commission web site provides information on broadcasting regulation and current issues at: http://www.fcc.com

More than a thousand news organizations, including most U.S. daily newspapers can be accessed at: http://www.newslink.org/menu.html

ANALYTICAL THINKING EXERCISES

A. Select at least three articles by syndicated columnists from a newspaper that address similar issues. Go through the articles and compare their points of view, applying some of the analytical thinking criteria presented in Chapter One of this *Study Guide.*

B. Make note of some of the most commonly read news magazines in your household including those that you favor. In the library reference section find *Magazines for Libraries* and look of the ideological rating for the magazines you have selected to review.

C. Apply the analytical thinking format from Chapter One of this *Study Guide* to a discussion of the reading "The Miscast Institution" by Thomas Patterson at the end of Chapter Ten.

TEST QUESTIONS FOR REVIEW

True/False

1. Over the course of American history, newspapers have become increasingly **more** partisan in their political coverage.

2. The *New York Times* has established itself as the national "newspaper of record."

3. Both newspaper publishers and broadcasters have been equally subjected to regulation by the federal government to assign service areas for coverage.

4. The term "agenda setter" is used to describe the news media's ability to influence what is on people's minds.

5. In general, the press is less interested in reporting on institutions such as Congress or the courts than on people.

6. The American media often offer the American people widely different versions of the news.

7. A reason why news organizations cannot function adequately in the role of public representative is that the press is more responsive to news opportunities than to political interests.

8. The news media is not equipped to help people actually solve political and social problems because the news media creates a "pseudocommunity" in America.

9. Objective journalism is based on reporting "facts" rather than relating the opinions of the writer.

10. The media differs from interest groups and political parties in that the media are more inclined to promote and defend particular specific interests.

Multiple Choice

1. The early press in the United States was most closely associated with:
a. weather and planting forecasts.
b. political partisanship.
c. advertising.
d. gossip.

2. The headline "Death of a Monster" exemplifies:
a. objective reporting.
b. partisan reporting.
c. sensationalist reporting.
d. muckraking journalism.

3. Objective reporting is based on the idea that a reporter's job is to:
a. report the facts in order to cover both sides of partisan debates.
b. report what political leaders want them to report.
c. discover what other reporters are saying and provide a uniform interpretation of events.
d. scrutinize partisan debates and tell the news audience which party has the better argument.

4. The lack of diversity in modern newspaper reporting compared with reporting in earlier historical eras is influenced by all except which one of the following:
a. federal regulatory policies.
b. a widespread move toward adoption of objective journalism.
c. national and international news services.
d. decreases in newspaper competition.

5. "On-the-scene" coverage of a natural disaster is an example of the press exercising which role:
a. watchdog.
b. public representative.
c. common-carrier.
d. signaler.

6. As part of its signaler role, the media also performs the function of:
a. protecting the public interest.
b. setting the public agenda.
c. investigating elected officials for wrongdoing.
d. influencing the behavior of politicians.

7. "Horse race journalism" refers primarily to media coverage of:
a. the stock market.
b. the sports world.
c. election campaigns.
d. legislative debates.

8. The first "national" news medium was:
a. large-circulation newspaper chains.
b. radio networks.
c. television networks.
d. cable television stations.

9. An example of the press exercising its role as watchdog is coverage of the:
a. O.J. Simpson trial.
b. U.S. military assistance to Bosnia.
c. U.S. involvement in the Persian Gulf War.
d. Watergate scandal.

10. Under FCC regulations, during campaigns broadcasters are required to:
a. give each candidate an equal amount of coverage.
b. charge candidates a market variable rate for air time.
c. not permit biased coverage especially during campaigns.
d. offer candidates the lowest rate for air time charged to commercial advertisers.

11. Public officials are **not** able to collect libel damages from negative news coverage if:
a. they can convincingly demonstrate that the news organization was false in its accusations.
b. they can show that the news media was careless in its search for truthful information.
c. the media can provide supporting evidence about an allegation made about an individual.
d. the news organization reported false material maliciously.

12. The media has made inroads into which role of political parties:
a. advocating the public interest.
b. nominating officials for public office.
c. fundraising for campaigns.
d. censoring behavior of public officials.

13. The style of reporting called "yellow journalism":
a. stressed factual coverage of events.
b. emphasized sensationalism to attract readers.
c. was subsidized by the major political parties.
d. was favored by government critics.

14. Application of First Amendment protections to the U.S. press has:
a. kept the press from reporting any "officials secrets."
b. barred the press from publishing any unsupported allegations about public officials.
c. discouraged news attacks on public officials.
d. enabled the government to block any news if it could convincingly demonstrate in court that publication of it would jeopardize national security.

15. The establishment of a cooperative relationship between a reporter and a public official can promote which role of the media?
a. signaler
b. public protector
c. common carrier
d. watchdog

Essays

1. Identify the four roles the media performs in current American politics, discussing which two roles you think are most crucial to protecting democracy.

2. Do you think the media encourages or discourages a mass-based participatory democracy? Why or why not?

3. Do you think that the way the media covers politicians and political events today is healthy or damaging to the public's image of American government?

4. Increasingly during political campaigns the media engages in what is called "negative reporting," which is in turn supported by campaign advertising that is personalized and negative. Despite what studies show about the "success" of this type of coverage, do you think it serves the public well in selecting the best candidates for office or does this type of coverage make any difference to an intelligent, well-informed voting public?

ANSWER KEY

True/False

1. F	3. F	5. T	7. T	9. T
2. T	4. T	6. F	8. T	10. F

Multiple Choice

1. b	4. a	7. c	10. d	13. b
2. c	5. d	8. b	11. c	14. d
3. a	6. b	9. d	12. a	15. c

CHAPTER ELEVEN
- CONGRESS -

LEARNING OBJECTIVES

After reading this chapter students should be able to:

1. Describe how the U.S. Congress serves as both a lawmaking and representative institution.
2. Describe what factors affect turnover rates for members of Congress.
3. Identify advantages and disadvantages of incumbency.
4. Define reapportionment and redistricting.
5. Describe the functions of leaders in Congress.
6. Describe how the principle of seniority works.
7. Name and describe the various types of committees in Congress.
8. Distinguish among the lawmaking, representation and oversight functions of Congress.
9. Describe the major steps in a bill becoming a law.

FOCUS AND MAIN POINTS

This chapter examines Congress, beginning with congressional elections and organization, and concludes with congressional policymaking. The following points are emphasized:

- Congressional elections tend to have a strong local orientation and to favor incumbents (particularly House members) who have traditionally had a substantial advantage in election campaigns.

- Although party leaders in Congress provide collective leadership, the work of Congress is done mainly through its committees and subcommittees, each of which has its separate leadership and policy jurisdiction.

- Congress lacks the direction and organization required for the development of comprehensive national policies, but is well organized to handle policies of relatively narrow scope. At times, Congress takes the lead on broad national issues but ordinarily does not do so.

CHAPTER SUMMARY

Members of Congress, once elected, are likely to be reelected. Members of Congress can use their office to publicize themselves, pursue a "service strategy" of responding to the needs of individual constituents, and secure pork barrel projects for their state or district. House members gain a greater advantage from these activities than do senators, whose larger constituencies make it harder for them to build close personal relations with voters and whose office is more likely to attract a strong challenger. Incumbency does have some disadvantages. Members of Congress must take positions on controversial issues, may blunder into a political scandal or indiscretion, must deal with changes in the electorate, or may face strong challengers. Any of these conditions can reduce their re-election chances. By and large, however, the advantages of incumbency outweigh the disadvantages, particularly for House members. Incumbents' advantages extend into their re-election campaigns. Their influential positions in Congress make it easier for them to raise campaign funds.

Congress is a fragmented institution. It has no single leader; the House and Senate have separate leaders, neither of whom can presume to speak for the other chamber. The principal party leaders of Congress are the Speaker of the House and the Senate majority leader. They share leadership power with committee and subcommittee chairpersons, who have influence on the policy decisions of their committee or subcommittee.

It is in committees that most of the day-to-day work of Congress is conducted. Each standing committee of the House and Senate has jurisdiction over congressional policy in a particular area (such as agriculture or foreign relations), as does each of its subcommittees. In most cases, the full House and Senate accept committee recommendations about passage of bills, although amendments to bills are quite common and committees are careful to take other members of Congress into account when making legislative decisions. Congress is a legislative system in which influence is widely dispersed, an arrangement that suits the power and re-election needs of its individual members. However, partisanship is a strong and binding force in Congress. It is the basis for party leaders' ability to build support for major legislative initiatives.

On this type of legislation, rather than committees, the party leaders and caucuses are the central actors.

The major function of Congress is to enact legislation. Yet the role it plays in developing legislation depends on the type of policy involved. Because of its divided chambers, weak leadership and committee structure as well as the concern of its members with state and district interests, Congress only occasionally takes the lead on broad national issues. Congress normally looks to the president for this leadership; nevertheless, presidential initiatives are passed by Congress only if they meet its members' expectations and usually only after a lengthy process of compromise and negotiation. Congress is more adept at handling legislation dealing with problems of narrow interest. Legislation of this sort is decided mainly in congressional committees where interested legislators, bureaucrats, and groups concentrate their efforts on issues of mutual concern.

A second function of Congress is the representation of various interests. Members of Congress are highly sensitive to the state or district they depend upon for re-election. Members of Congress do respond to overriding national interests but for most of them, local concerns generally come first. National and local representation often work through party representation, particularly on issues that divide the Democratic and Republican parties and their constituent groups.

Congress's third function is oversight, which involves the supervision and investigation of the way the bureaucracy is implementing legislatively mandated programs. Although oversight is a difficult process, it is an important means of control over the actions of the executive branch.

MAJOR CONCEPTS

bill--a proposed law (legislative act) within Congress or another legislature.

cloture--a parliamentary maneuver which, if a three-fifths majority votes for it, limits Senate debate to 100 hours and has the effect of defeating a filibuster.

conference committee--a temporary committee that is formed to bargain over the differences in the House and Senate versions of a bill. The committee's members are usually appointed from the House and Senate standing committees that originally worked on the bill.

constituency--the individuals who live within the geographical area represented by an elected official. More narrowly, the body of citizens eligible to vote for a particular representative.

filibuster--a procedural tactic in the U.S. Senate whereby a minority of legislators prevent a bill from coming to a vote by holding the floor and talking until the majority gives in and the bill is withdrawn from consideration.

gerrymandering--process by which one party draws district boundaries to its advantage.

jurisdiction (of a congressional committee)--the policy area in which a particular congressional committee is authorized to act.

law (as enacted by Congress)--a legislative proposal, or bill, that is passed by both the House and Senate and is either signed or not vetoed by the president.

lawmaking function--the authority (of a legislature) to make the laws necessary to carry out the government's powers.

oversight function--a supervisory activity of Congress that centers on its constitutional responsibility to see that the executive carries out the laws faithfully and spends appropriations properly.

party caucus--party organization within Congress consisting of a separate and distinct group for members of each political party from which party leaders are selected and party interests defined.

party discipline--the ability of a party's House or Senate members to act together as a cohesive group to support major party objectives.

party leaders--members of the House and Senate who are chosen by the Democratic or Republican caucus in each chamber to represent the party's interests in that chamber and who give some central direction to the chamber's deliberations.

pork barrel projects--laws whose tangible benefits are targeted at a particular legislator's constituency.

reapportionment--the process, after a new population census, of redistributing House seats so that the number of seats in each state more closely reflects the size of each state's population.

redistricting--the process of altering election districts in order to make them as nearly equal in population as possible. Redistricting takes place every ten years, after each population census.

representation function--the responsibility of a legislature to represent various interests in society.

rider--an amendment to a bill being considered by Congress.

seniority--a member of Congress's consecutive years of service on a particular committee.

service strategy--use of personal staff by members of Congress to perform services for constituents in order to gain their support in future elections.

standing committee--a permanent congressional committee with responsibility for a particular area of public policy. An example is the Senate Foreign Relations Committee.

sunset law--an oversight device which fixes a date on which a program will end unless it is renewed by Congress.

veto--presidential refusal to sign a bill whereby the bill is sent back to its originating chamber with the president's reasons for not signing it.

BOXES, TABLES AND FIGURES IN THE TEXT

Boxes
>How the U.S. Compares: Unity and Fragmentation In National
>Legislatures
>States in the Nation: One Person, One Vote? Not in Election of Senators

Tables
>The Standing Committees of Congress

Figures
>Reelection Rates of House Incumbents
>Congressional Campaign Expenditures
>Allocation of PAC Contributions Between Incumbents and Challengers in
>Congressional Races That Included an Incumbent, 1972-2000
>How a Bill Becomes a Law
>Percentage of Roll-Call Votes in House and Senate in Which a Majority of
>Democrats Voted Against a Majority of Republicans, 1970-1996.

INTERNET RESOURCES

A great deal of information is available both through Gopher sites and Web pages about Congress in general, legislation, members of Congress and activities of both the House and the Senate.

For information about congressional floor activity, committees and historical documents, access Thomas at: http://www.thomas.loc.gov.

The Library of Congress can be located at: http://www.loc.gov.

Congress uses the General Accounting Office to investigate and audit all federally financed programs. It can be accessed at: http://www.gao.gov.

Project Vote Smart information on Congress is found at: http://www.vote-smart.org/congress/congress.html.

Congressional Quarterly Gopher service is found at gopher://gopher.cqalert.com.

The Web server for the U.S. House of Representatives can be found at: http://www.house.gov and the Senate at http://www.senate.gov.

You can use your mail zip code to identify your Congressional representative through http://www.voxpop.org/zipper/

If you want to compare your own views with those of your representative, see: http://pnl.politicsnow.com/interact/ctr/

For a comparative look at the operations of the British Parliament, access: http://www.parliament.uk/

For current developments within Congress look at the online version of Roll Call--the newspaper of Capitol Hill. Locate it at: http://congress.nw.dc.us/rollcall

Spending for pork barrel projects is tracked by the Washington-based Citizens Against Government Waste. Their site is located at: http://www.cagw.org

ANALYTICAL THINKING EXERCISES

A. Based on the information provided in Figure 11-5, what legislative strategy would you think that the president would pursue? If you were a House member from the party opposite from the president, what strategy for proposing and passing legislation would you pursue?

B. Apply the analytical thinking format provided in Chapter One of this *Study Guide* to the essay "Tammany Hall Goes to Washington" by Morris P. Fiorina at the end of Chapter Eleven in the text.

TEST QUESTIONS FOR REVIEW

True/False

1. Safe incumbency in which candidates of one party are virtually assured of elections are more prevalent in the Senate than in the House.

2. Most of the legislative decisions in Congress are made, in effect, by committees and subcommittees rather than by the entire House and Senate.

3. The U.S. Congress is characterized by strong party unity.

4. The President of the Senate is also the Vice-President of the U.S. Committee chairs are selected by seniority regardless of their political party identification.

5. The political party with the majority of seats in Congress also holds the majority of seats on each committee and subcommittee.

6. Although Congress looks to the president for policy leadership on national issues, it does not quickly accept most legislative proposals developed in the White House.

7. Partisan identifications are no longer a significant predictor of how members of Congress will vote.

8. Congressional oversight is the process by which the full House or Senate keeps track of the work of its committees.

9. When faced with a strong conflict between what is best for the nation and what is best for their local constituency, most members of Congress would likely respond to local needs.

Multiple Choice

1. The term "service strategy" refers to the:
a. use of congressional staff to build support among constituents.
b. tendency of members of Congress to back the president on crucial issues of national security.
c. tendency of the armed services to cater to members of Congress.
d. desire of members of Congress to focus on re-election in order to accumulate the years required for good seniority positions.

2. The primary source of campaign funds for congressional election campaigns is:
a. personal funds.
b. political action committees.
c. individual donations.
d. national government funds.

3. Compared with the Senate majority leader, the Speaker of the House has more power because the House:
a. places fewer restrictions on floor debate allowing a filibuster.
b. is the larger of the two chambers in terms of membership.
c. has less of a tradition as "a chamber of equals."
d. b and c only.
e. a, b and c.

4. Which of the following is not a Congressional agency?
a. General Accounting Office
b. Congressional Budget Office
c. Office of Management and Budget
d. Office of Technology Assessment

5. Unlimited debate employed in the Senate to keep a bill from coming up for a vote is called:
a. pork-barreling legislation.
b. mark-up strategy.
c. filibuster.
d. log rolling.

6. Measures enacted to prevent a program from continuing forever are called:
a. mark-ups.
b. sunset laws.
c. cloture.
d. legislative vetoes.

7. On broad issues of national significance, who usually takes the initiative to propose legislative initiatives?
a. president.
b. special interest groups.
c. party of the president in Congress.
d. congressional staff of the minority party.

8. What is the name of the type of committee that reconciles different House and Senate versions of a bill?
a. standing
b. special
c. conference
d. joint

9. The major function of the U.S. Congress is to:
a. pass legislation.
b. administer programs.
c. decide exceptions to the enforcement of laws.
d. nominate candidates for national office.
e. a and c only.

10. General descriptive characteristics of the U.S. Congress include all except which one of the following:
a. Congress is a fragmented (highly decentralized) institution.
b. Influence in Congress is widely dispersed.
c. Congress most often takes the lead in handling broad national issues.
d. Most work is conducted in committees.
e. Both the House and Senate are directly elected by the populace.

11. The text description of the NAFTA vote illustrates which aspect(s) of Congress? Its:
a. lawmaking powers.
b. power of incumbency.
c. role as a representative assembly for states and districts.
d. a and b only.
e. a and c only.

12. The Speaker of the U.S. House of Representatives can:
a. veto major legislation from the office of the president.
b. choose members of the House Rules Committee.
c. recognize people from the floor of Congress to speak on a bill.
d. a and c only.
e. b and c only.

13. The practice of sending an agricultural bill to the Foreign Relations committee instead of the Agriculture committee for deliberation would offend the policy of:
a. seniority.
b. cloture.
c. log rolling.
d. jurisdiction

14. When Congress passes a "distributive" piece of legislation, it means:
a. benefits are taken away from one group and given to another.
b. benefits are distributed to a particular group while spreading the costs among the general public.
c. benefits are distributed equally among the population.
d. costs and benefits are distributed equally among the general public.

15. Congressional investigations such as Watergate, Iran-Contra and Whitewater illustrate which function of Congress?
a. representation
b. lawmaking
c. distributive
d. oversight
e. service

Essays

1. In a clash between the executive branch and the legislative branch over an issue such as the U.S. budget, what powers can Congress bring to bear to influence the executive branch? What are some limits to its ability to get its way?

2. Given legislative gridlock problems in recent years, do you think the time has come for the United States to seriously consider a switch to a parliamentary system of government such as exists in some of the European democracies? Discuss.

3. If you were going to run for either the U.S. House or Senate, what factors would you need to take into account and what election strategy would you pursue?

4. Since only about 10% of the bills that are introduced in Congress get passed, what elements mentioned in your text contribute to the difficulty of getting a bill out of committee and brought up for a successful vote on the floor.

ANSWER KEY

True/False

1. F	3. F	5. F	7. T	9. F
2. T	4. T	6. T	8. F	

Multiple Choice

1. a	4. c	7. a	10. c	13. d
2. c	5. c	8. c	11. e	14. b
3. d	6. b	9. a	12. e	15. d

CHAPTER TWELVE
- THE PRESIDENCY -

LEARNING OBJECTIVES

After reading this chapter students should be able to:

1. Name and identify the basic constitutional powers given to the president.
2. Discuss additional powers assumed by presidents and the events that gave rise to them.
3. Identify various leadership roles presidents can adopt.
4. Describe the role of the Electoral College in electing presidents.
5. Identify some objects of the presidential nomination process.
6. Generally describe the role played by money and the media in contemporary presidential campaigns.
7. Assess the effects of staffing on presidents' control of executive authority.
8. Discuss how the executive branch can set policy independently of Congress.
9. Identify ways to limit executive power.
10. Describe connections between presidential approval ratings and a president's ability to lead effectively.

FOCUS AND MAIN POINTS

The presidency has become a more powerful office than the Framers envisioned, primarily because of two features of the office--national elections and singular authority--which have enabled presidents to make use of changing demands on government to expand the presidential leadership role. This chapter explores this development and then examines the presidential selection process and the staffing of the modern presidency, both of which contribute to the president's prominence in the American political system. The chapter concludes with an examination of the presidential role in policymaking and some factors that contribute to success or failure in that realm.

The main ideas of the chapter are these:

Changing national and world conditions have required the presidency to become a strong office; underlying this development are the constitution's flexibility regarding the presidency and the public support the president acquires from being the only nationally elected official.

The modern presidential election campaign is a marathon affair in which self-selected candidates must plan for a strong start in the nominating contests and center their general election strategies on media and a baseline of party support.

The modern presidency could not operate without a large staff of assistants, experts and high-level managers, but the sheer size of this staff makes it impossible for the president to exercise complete control over it.

A president's election by national vote and his position as sole chief executive ensure that others will listen to his ideas; to succeed, however, the president must get others to respond to his leadership.

CHAPTER SUMMARY

The presidency has become a much stronger office than the Framers envisioned. The Constitution grants presidents substantial military, diplomatic, legislative and executive powers, and in each case presidential authority has increased measurably. Underlying this change is the president's position as the one leader chosen by the whole nation and as the sole head of the executive branch. These features of the office have enabled presidents to claim broad authority in response to increased demands on the federal government by changing world and national conditions.

During the course of American history, the presidential selection process has been altered in ways that were intended to make it more responsive to the preferences of ordinary people. Today, citizens vote not only in general elections but in selection of nominees. To gain nomination, a presidential hopeful must gain the support of the electorate in state primaries and open caucuses. Once nominated, candidates receive federal funds for their general election campaigns, which are based on televised appeals.

Although campaigns tend to personalize the presidency, the responsibilities of the modern presidency far exceed any president's personal capacities. To meet their obligations, presidents have surrounded themselves with large staffs of advisers, policy experts and managers. These staff members enable the president to extend control over the executive branch while providing him with information necessary for policymaking. All recent presidents have discovered, however, that their control of staff resources is incomplete and that some tasks done by others on their behalf actually work against what the president is trying to accomplish.

As the nation's sole chief executive and top elected leader, a president can expect that his policy and leadership efforts will receive attention. However, other institutions, particularly Congress, have the authority to make this leadership effective. No president has come close to winning approval for all programs he has placed before Congress, but presidents' records of success have varied considerably. Factors contributing to a president's success include national conditions requiring strong White House leadership and having the president's party hold a majority in Congress.

To retain an effective leadership position, presidents depend on the backing of the American people. Recent presidents have made extensive use of the media to build support for their programs. Many have had difficulty maintaining that support throughout their terms of office. A major reason is that the public expects far more from its presidents than they can deliver.

MAJOR CONCEPTS

Cabinet--a group consisting of the heads of the (cabinet) executive departments, who are appointed by the president, subject to confirmation by the Senate. The cabinet was once the main advisory body to the president but no longer plays this role.

honeymoon period--the president's first months in office, a time when Congress, the press and the public are more inclined than usual to support presidential initiatives.

legitimacy--the idea that the choice of a president should be based on the will of the people as expressed through their votes.

momentum--a strong showing by a candidate in early presidential nominating contests, which leads to a buildup of public support for the candidate.

open party caucuses--meetings at which a party's candidates for nomination are voted upon and which are open to all of the party's rank-and-file voters who want to attend.

presidential approval rating--a measure of the degree to which the public approves or disapproves of a president's performance in office.

stewardship theory--a theory that argues for a strong, assertive presidential role, with presidential authority limited only at points specifically prohibited by law.

unit rule--all of a state's electoral votes are awarded to the candidate who wins the state's popular vote.

Whig theory--a nineteenth century theory that the presidency was a limited or restrained office whose occupant was confined to expressly granted constitutional authority.

BOXES, TABLES AND FIGURES IN THE TEXT

INTERNET RESOURCES

To access the White House on the Web, type in : http://www.whitehouse.gov.
From this site you can connect to more than 25 executive agencies and to the Voice of
America.

All cabinet departments can be found at:
http://www.whitehouse.gov/WH/Cabinet/html/cabinet_links.html

Presidential addresses can be found at: http://www.law.uoknor.edu/ushist.html

Another way to get information about the government as well as to link up with other
government servers is through FedWorld at http://www.fedworld.gov.

The Federal Web Locator can be found at http://www.law.vill.edu/fed-
agency/fedwebloc.html

This site has general information on specific presidents and links to the presidential
libraries: http://sunsite.unc.edu:80/lia/president

Profiles of the nation's presidents, their cabinet officers, and key events during their
time in office can be found at: http://www.ipl.org/ref/POTUS

Contact Vote Smart for information on the presidency and the Executive Office of the
President as well as links to key executive agencies and organizations:
http://www.vote-smart.org/executive

ANALYTICAL THINKING EXERCISES

A. Looking at Figure 12-3 regarding percentage of bills passed by Congress on
which the president announced a position. Note two presidents with the most
and least success. Are there any presidents who were successful when their
political party did not control Congress? What is the success rate when the
president's party controls only one chamber of Congress?

B. Use the analytical thinking format in Chapter One of this *Study Guide* to discuss "The Postmodern President" by Richard Rose at the end of Chapter Twelve in the text.

C. Box 12-4 presents some information on impeaching, convicting, and removing the president. Apply these criteria to the impeachment proceedings against Andrew Johnson, Richard Nixon, and Bill Clinton.
You might seek information for this exercise from appropriate web-sites.

D. After consulting Box 12-1 on the Electoral College, formulate a position on whether to reform or abolish it. You may want to get more information from a web-site such as: http://www.state.ma.us/sec/ele/elecoll/collidx.htm

TEST QUESTIONS FOR REVIEW

True/False

1. In practice, the presidency is a more powerful office than the Framers envisioned it would be under the Constitution.

2. The Whig theory of the presidency calls for limited use of powers based on expressly granted constitutional authority.

3. A key to success in presidential nomination campaigns is "momentum."

4. The electoral vote for president has always been tied to the popular vote.

5. The Constitution very clearly gives the vice-president responsibility over some areas of executive authority.

6. Historically, presidents have put forth most of their program initiatives early in their administrations.

7. Significant presidential action can often succeed without the approval of Congress, the cooperation of the bureaucracy and sometimes the acceptance of the judiciary.

8. The War Powers Act was passed to curb presidential authority.

9. The presidency is unique among American elected officials because presidents can claim to represent the whole nation.

10. Presidential success is related to party support in Congress.

Multiple Choice

1. The president's constitutional roles, such as chief executive and commander-in-chief:
a. are based on very precise and unchangeable constitutional grants of power.
b. are rooted in tradition only; they are not included in the Constitution.
c. are not shared with Congress.
d. have been extended in practice to be more powerful than the writers of the Constitution intended.

2. Which of the following reforms was achieved by Andrew Jackson:
a. abolition of the Electoral College.
b. elimination of the caucus process for nominating candidates.
c. use of the national political party nominating convention.
d. use of primary elections to nominate candidates.

3. The president's role as domestic policy leader became increasingly important after the 19th century because of:
a. the nation's shift from an agrarian to an industrial society, which placed substantial new demands on government.
b. changes in mass communications.
c. a shift in Congress toward local concerns rather than national ones.
d. women and minorities demanding policies that supported their interests.

4. The source of most presidential campaign funds for major party candidates is:
a. PAC money.
b. federal funding.
c. contributions from individual citizens.
d. the candidate's personal funds.

5. By tradition, the choice of the vice-presidential nomination rests with:
a. delegates to the national nominating convention.
b. congressional leaders.
c. the presidential nominee.
d. electors especially chosen for the vice-presidential nomination.

6. Presidential staffing appointees who serve most closely with the president as personal advisers are in the:
a. White House Office.
b. Cabinet.
c. National Security Council.
d. Office of Management and Budget.

7. Which of the following contributes to successful presidential terms of office:
a. the margin of electoral victory.
b. partisan control of Congress.
c. existence of a compelling national problem.
d. b and c only.
e. a, b and c.

8. A president's policy initiatives are significantly more successful when the president:
a. has strong support from the American people.
b. is a former member of Congress.
c. is on good terms with other world leaders.
d. is in office when the economy goes bad, which demands stronger leadership.

9. The highest point of public support for a president is likely to occur:
a. during the president's first year in office.
b. after re-election to a second term.
c. immediately after Congress enacts a major presidential initiative.
d. when international conditions are stable.

10. In order to be elected president, what is the minimum number of electoral votes a presidential candidate must win?
a. 538
b. 353
c. 270
d. 435

11. The irony of modern day presidential government in the U.S. is that:
a. the public is most forgiving of presidential mistakes.
b. because the public expects so much from presidents, they get too little credit when things go well and too little blame when things go badly.
c. the president is weaker than Congress, yet must appear to be stronger.
d. the presidential office grows weaker as problems mount: just when the country could most use effective leadership, that leadership is often hardest to achieve.

12. The way the president can make diplomatic agreements with other nations yet by-pass formal Senate approval is by using the:
a. legislative veto.
b. executive agreement.
c. sunset laws.
d. power to make war.

13. The president's ability to take the lead in domestic policy in the early part of the 20th century developed from:
a. control over making up the national budget.
b. capacity to respond to national economic emergencies.
c. the need for national rather than local solutions to problems.
d. c and b only.
e. a, b and c.

14. The Federal Election Campaign Act of 1974 (with amendments) provides:
a. federal campaign funds for presidential primaries.
b. federal funds only for the winner of each state primary.
c. rigid regulations on the way campaigns are styled.
d. that the winner of the electoral vote becomes president.

15. The large number of bureaucratic agencies and appointees creates what problem(s) for presidents:
1. finding sources of information on issues.
2. using a collective decision-making style.
3. finding enough highly qualified people to nominate.
4. gaining control over their activities.
a. 1 and 2.   b. 2 and 3.   c. 3 and 4.   d. 2 and 4.   e. 1 and 3.

Essays

1. All American presidents since George Washington have entered office with essentially the same job description from Article II of the Constitution. What factors can you identify that affect differences in style and evaluation of presidents?

2. What are the four systems for presidential selection described by the text in Table 12-1. Looking at the time periods and major features, identify some patterns in presidential selection. Present some arguments for keeping the current process or for making further changes.

3. Do you think the present method for selecting American presidents is designed to attract the type of person needed for that position of leadership? Why or why not? Would you make any changes?

4. Some parliamentary democracies select their chief executive from the membership of the legislature thereby ensuring that there is a large enough legislative coalition to support the programs of the winning political party. Describe other differences between parliamentary and presidential systems and discuss whether you think reform of the American system is needed.

ANSWER KEY

True/False

1. T	3. T	5. F	7. F	9. T
2. T	4. F	6. T	8. T	10. T

Multiple Choice

1. d	4. b	7. e	10. c	13. e
2. c	5. c	8. a	11. d	14. a
3. a	6. a	9. a	12. b	15. d

CHAPTER THIRTEEN
- THE BUREAUCRACY -

LEARNING OBJECTIVES

After reading this chapter students should be able to:

1. Describe the general function of the bureaucracy.
2. Differentiate among cabinet departments, independent agencies and regulatory agencies.
3. Define hierarchical authority.
4. Differentiate among patronage, merit and executive leadership systems for staffing a bureaucracy.
5. Describe an "agency point of view."
6. Identify how bureaucratic agencies are held accountable for their activities.
7. Discuss the inherent conflict between bureaucratic power and democratic values.
8. Discuss the pros and cons of reforming the bureaucracy.

FOCUS AND MAIN POINTS

This chapter describes the nature of the federal bureaucracy and the politics surrounding it. The discussion initially aims at clarifying the bureaucracy's responsibilities, organizational structure and management practices. Also discussed is how the bureaucracy fits in the political game. Bureaucrats necessarily and naturally take an "agency point of view," seeking to promote their agency's objectives. The three constitutional branches of government impose a degree of accountability on the bureaucracy, but the sheer size and fragmented nature of the U.S. government confound the problem of control and make efforts to reform the bureaucracy a high priority. Primary points discussed in this chapter are the following:

*   Modern government could not function without a large bureaucracy; through hierarchy, specialization and rules, a bureaucratic form is the only practical way of organizing large-scale government programs.

- America's bureaucracy is expected simultaneously to respond to the direction of partisan officials and to administer programs fairly and competently. These conflicting demands are addressed through a combination of personnel management systems--the patronage, merit and executive leadership systems.

- Bureaucrats naturally take an "agency point of view," which they promote through their expert knowledge, support from clientele groups and backing by Congress or the president.

- Although agencies are subject to scrutiny by the president, Congress and the judiciary, bureaucrats are able to achieve power in their own right.

CHAPTER SUMMARY

Bureaucracy is a method of organizing people and work; it is based on the principles of hierarchical authority, job specialization and formalized rules. As a form of organization, bureaucracy is the most efficient means of getting people to work together on tasks of great magnitude and complexity. It is also a form of organization that is prone to waste and rigidity, which is why efforts are being made to "reinvent" it.

The United States could not be governed without a large federal bureaucracy. The day-to-day work of the federal government, from mail delivery to provision of social security to international diplomacy is accomplished by the bureaucracy. Federal employees work in roughly 400 major agencies, including cabinet departments, independent agencies, regulatory agencies, government corporations and presidential commissions. Yet the bureaucracy is more than simply an administrative giant. Administrators exercise considerable discretion in their policy decisions. In the process of implementing policy, they make important policy and political choices.

Each agency of the federal government was created in response to political demands on national officials. Because of its origins in political demands, the administration of government is necessarily political. An inherent conflict results from two simultaneous but incompatible demands on the bureaucracy: that it respond to the demands of partisan officials but also that it administer programs fairly and competently. These tensions are evident in the three concurrent personnel management systems under which the bureaucracy operates: patronage, merit and executive leadership.

Administrators are actively engaged in politics and policymaking. The fragmentation of power and the pluralism of the American political system result in a policy process that is continually subject to conflict and contention. There is no clear policy or leadership mandate in the American system, and hence government agencies must compete for the power required to administer their programs effectively. Accordingly, civil servants tend to have an agency point of view: they seek to advance their agency's programs and to repel attempts by others to weaken their position. In promoting their agency, civil servants rely on their policy expertise, the backing of their clientele groups, and support from the president and Congress.

Because administrators are not elected by the people they serve yet wield substantial independent power, the bureaucracy's accountability is a major issue. Major checks on the bureaucracy are provided by the president, Congress and the courts. President have some power to reorganize the bureaucracy and authority to appoint political heads of agencies. Presidents also have management tools (such as the executive budget) that can be used to limit administrators' discretion. Congress has influence on bureaucratic agencies through its authorization and funding powers and through various devices (including sunset laws and oversight hearings) that hold administrators accountable for their actions. The judiciary's role in ensuring the bureaucracy's accountability is smaller than that of the elected branches, but the courts do have the authority to force agencies to act in accordance with legislative intent, established procedures, and constitutionally guaranteed rights. Nevertheless, administrators are not fully accountable. They exercise substantial independent power, a situation that is not easily reconciled with democratic values.

Efforts are currently under way to scale down the federal bureaucracy. This reduction includes cuts in budgets, staff and organizational units, and also involves changes in the way the bureaucracy does its work. This process is a response to both political forces and new management theories.

MAJOR CONCEPTS

accountability--the ability of the public to hold government officials responsible for their actions.

agency point of view-the tendency of bureaucrats to place the interests of their agency ahead of other interests and ahead of the priorities sought by the president or Congress.

bureaucracy--a system of organization and control based on the principles of hierarchical authority, job specialization and formalized rules.

cabinet (executive) departments--the major administrative organizations within the federal executive bureaucracy, each of which is headed by a secretary (cabinet officer) and has responsibility for a major function of the federal government, such as defense, agriculture or justice.

clientele groups--special-interest groups that benefit directly from the activities of a particular bureaucratic agency and are therefore strong advocates of the agency.

demographic representativeness--the idea that the bureaucracy will be more responsive to the public if its employees at all levels are demographically representative of the population as a whole.

executive leadership system--an approach to managing the bureaucracy that is based on presidential leadership and presidential management tools such as the president's annual budget proposal.

formalized rules--a basic principle of bureaucracy that refers to the standardized procedures and established regulations by which a bureaucracy conducts its operations.

government corporations--bodies, such as the U.S. Postal Service and Amtrak, that are similar to private corporations in that they charge for their services but different in that they receive federal funding to help defray expenses. Their directors are appointed by the president with Senate approval.

hierarchical authority--a basic principle of bureaucracy that refers to the chain of command within an organization whereby officials and units have control over those below them.

independent agencies--bureaucratic agencies that are similar to cabinet departments but usually have a narrower area of responsibility. Each such agency is headed by a presidential appointee who is not a cabinet member. An example is the National Aeronautics and Space Administration (NASA).

job specialization--a basic principle of bureaucracy which holds that the responsibilities of each job position should be explicitly defined and that a precise division of labor within the organization should be maintained.

merit (civil service) system--an approach to managing the bureaucracy whereby people are appointed to government positions on the basis of either competitive examinations or special qualifications, such as professional training.

neutral competence--the administrative objective of a merit-based bureaucracy. Such a bureaucracy should be "competent" in the sense that its employees are hired and retained on the basis of their expertise and "neutral" in the sense that it operates by objective standards rather than partisan ones.

patronage system--an approach to managing the bureaucracy whereby people are appointed to important government positions as a reward for political services they have rendered and because of their partisan loyalty.

policy implementation--the primary function of the bureaucracy is policy implementation, which refers to the process of carrying out of the authoritative decisions of Congress, the president and the courts.

presidential commissions--these organizations within the bureaucracy are headed by commissioners appointed by the president. An example of such a commission is the Commission on Civil Rights.

regulatory agencies--administrative units, such as the Federal Communications Commission and the Environmental Protection Agency, that have responsibility for monitoring and regulating ongoing economic activities.

spoils system--the practice of granting public office to individuals in return for political favors they have rendered.

whistle-blowing--an internal check on the bureaucracy whereby individual bureaucrats report instances of mismanagement that they observe.

BOXES, TABLES AND FIGURES IN THE TEXT

Boxes
> How the U.S. Compares: Educational Backgrounds of Bureaucrats
> States in the Nation: The Size of State Bureaucracies

Tables
> Selected U.S. Regulatory Agencies, Independent Agencies, Government Corporations, and Presidential Commissions
> Strengths and Weaknesses of Major Systems for Managing the Bureaucracy
> Federal Job Rankings (GS) of Various Demographic Groups

Figures
> Cabinet (Executive) Departments
> Number of Persons Employed by the Federal Government, 1791-1996
> The Public Confidence in the Bureaucracy

INTERNET RESOURCES

Use FedWorld to find government information, department reports and links to departments: http://www.fedworld.gov/

To locate the web site for the FBI: http://www.fbi.gov/; for FCC: www.fcc.gov/

To have input into the bureaucracy, type: http://www.2020vision.org/admin.html

For information on reforming the bureaucracy, enter: http://www.npr.gov

The Bureau of Labor Statistics can be found at: http://stats.bls.gov

The Census Bureau has a home page at http://www.census.gov

Contact the Government Accountability Project which is designed to protect and encourage whistleblowers by providing information and support to federal employees at: http://www.whistleblower.org

For a list of the cabinet secretaries and links to each cabinet-level department see: http://www.whitehouse.gov/WH/Cabinet

A site for those interested in finding employment with the federal government which provides job application and other information for the various federal agencies can be contacted at: http://iccweb.com/federal

ANALYTICAL THINKING EXERCISES

A. Look at the box on "Educational Backgrounds of Bureaucrats" and the consequences of hiring employees with different backgrounds. Notice where the United States places in the hiring of college majors. Describe some changes in emphasis that might develop if hiring practices were changed. Would you favor some of these changes that might result?

B. Use the analytical thinking format in Chapter One of this *Study Guide* to discuss "Reinventing Government" by David Osborne and Ted Gaebler at the end of Chapter Thirteen of your text.

TEST QUESTIONS FOR REVIEW

True/False

1. The main effect of formalized rules within bureaucratic organizations is to create the "red tape" that gives bureaucrats their power over other political actors.

2. Hierarchy is intended to increase the speed of bureaucratic decision-making by reducing conflict over the power to make decisions.

3. Federal employees are forbidden by law to join labor unions.

4. Independent agencies differ from executive departments in that they are not granted responsibility for specific policy areas.

5. Most legislation contains general policy goals, leaving bureaucrats to decide the specific means by which to accomplish these goals.

6. All federal government positions are filled according to merit system criteria.

7. The SEC and EPA are examples of regulatory agencies.

8. Most bureaucratic agencies have an antagonistic relationship with the interest groups that depend on the programs they run.

9. Advocates of a demographically representative bureaucracy claim that such a bureaucracy would be a more accountable one.

10. The agency point of view is characteristic of middle-rank civil servants but not high-ranking ones.

Multiple Choice

1. The Post Office and Amtrak are examples of:
a. private corporations.
b. government corporations.
c. independent agencies.
d. regulatory agencies.

2. Whenever Congress has perceived a need for close and continuous control of an economic activity, it has tended to create a:
a. cabinet department.
b. presidential commission.
c. government corporation.
d. regulatory agency.

3. "Street-level" bureaucracy as described by Lipsky refers to the discretion used by lower level officials in the:
a. initiation of policy.
b. development of policy.
c. delivery of services.
d. evaluation of programs.

4. The federal bureaucracy's policy responsibilities include:
a. not going beyond the administration of policy.
b. exercising discretion in policy in a few highly restricted areas.
c. exemption from discretion in carrying out its policy responsibilities.
d. not simply administering policy but making it as well.

5. The modern civil service system is based on:
a. informal standards of ability for people doing specific tasks.
b. codified classifications and prerequisite experience or competitive testing.
c. promotion and salary commensurate with partisan policy activity.
d. executive selection from a field of equally qualified applicants.

6. The administrative concept of neutral competence holds that the bureaucracy should:
a. be staffed by people chosen on the basis of ability and who work fairly on behalf of all citizens.
b. stay out of conflicts between Congress and the president.
c. be structured on the basis of the principles of specialization, hierarchy and formal rules.
d. not permit in-fighting between agencies.

7. The chief goal of the executive leadership system is:
a. the shifting of power from Congress to the president.
b. the establishment of partisanship as the basis for the administration of policy.
c. improved coordination among the bureaucracy's programs and agencies.
d. a better system for training entry level bureaucrats.

8. Three terms from your text that best characterize bureaucracy are:
a. hierarchy, specialization and rules.
b. inefficiency, inflexibility and red tape.
c. honesty, efficiency and patronage.
d. corruption, incompetence and spoils.

9. Responsibility for oversight of the bureaucracy belongs chiefly to the:
a. Congress.
b. president.
c. courts.
d. press.

10. In promoting their agency's goals, bureaucrats rely on:
1. their expert knowledge.
2. the backing of the president and Congress.
3. the support of interests that benefit from the agency's programs.
4. judicial support.
a. 2 and 4.   b. 1, 3, 4.   c. 2, 3, 4.   d. 1, 2, 3.   e. all the above.

11. The final authority to approve or disapprove an agency's budget lies with the:
a. cabinet secretary.
b. Congress.
c. president.
d. OMB.

12. Iron triangles typically involve all except which one of the following:
a. bureaucratic agencies.
b. White House aides.
c. clientele groups.
d. congressional subcommittees.

13. Which of the following groups cannot limit the power of the bureaucracy?
a. the president
b. Congress
c. the electorate
d. the judiciary
e. political parties

14. The appeal of bureaucracy as a form of organization is that it:
a. increases unnecessary duplication of tasks.
b. can only be used in the private sector.
c. allows individuals great latitude in completing a task.
d. is the most efficient means of getting people to work together on tasks of great magnitude.

15. Which of the following is **not** a criticism of the federal bureaucracy:
a. It is rigid and costly.
b. It enables modern government to undertake large and ambitious programs.
c. It is not directly accountable to the American people.
d. Its size and fragmentation make it hard to control.
e. b and c only.

Essays

1. In what ways can the president, Congress and judiciary keep the bureaucracy accountable to the American people? What are the disadvantages of not being able to control the bureaucracy?

2. The text asserts that the federal bureaucracy today embodies aspects of all three systems of staffing as outlined from Table 13-2. Summarize from that table the strengths and weakness of each system, drawing conclusions about the effective composition of a bureaucracy for the future.

3. Identify and discuss the favorable and unfavorable factors to be considered in current day plans under the concept of reinventing government to reform the federal bureaucracy. How can the bureaucracy be responsive to the public with reductions in its budgets, staff and organizational units?

4. Do you think it is true that Congress through iron triangles and issue networks uses the bureaucracy to reward its supporters? Why or why not?

ANSWER KEY

True/False

1. F	3. F	5. T	7. T	9. T
2. T	4. F	6. F	8. F	10. F

Multiple Choice

1. b	4. d	7. c	10. d	13. c
2. d	5. b	8. a	11. b	14. d
3. c	6. a	9. a	12. b	15. b

CHAPTER FOURTEEN
- THE JUDICIARY -

LEARNING OBJECTIVES

After reading this chapter students should be able to:

1. Distinguish between the jurisdictions of state and federal court systems.
2. Identify the criteria a state law case must meet to be considered in the federal court system.
3. Differentiate between trial and appellate courts.
4. Discuss the role partisan politics plays in the selection of federal judges.
5. Identify the political factors that influence Supreme Court decision making.
6. Describe what the issues of legitimacy and compliance entail and how they effect the Supreme Court's policymaking process.
7. Distinguish between the doctrines of judicial restraint and activism.

FOCUS AND MAIN POINTS

This chapter describes the federal judiciary and the work of its judges and justices. Like the executive and legislative branches, the judiciary is an independent branch of the U.S. government, but, unlike the two other branches, its top officials are not elected by the people. The judiciary is not a democratic institution, and its role is different from and, in some areas, more controversial than those of the executive and legislative branches. Main points made in this chapter are the following:

- The federal judiciary includes the Supreme Court of the United States, which functions mainly as an appellate court; courts of appeal, which hear appeals; and district courts, which hold trials. States have court systems of their own, which for the most part are independent of federal court supervision.

- Judicial decisions are constrained by applicable constitutional law, statutory law and precedent. Nevertheless, political factors have a major influence on judicial appointments and decisions; judges are political officials as well as legal ones.

- The judiciary has become an increasingly powerful policymaking body in recent decades, which has raised questions regarding the judiciary's proper role in a democracy.

CHAPTER SUMMARY

At the lowest level of the federal judicial system are the district courts, where most federal cases begin. Above them are the federal courts of appeal, which review cases appealed from lower courts. The U.S. Supreme Court is the nation's highest court. Each state has its own court system, consisting of trial courts at the bottom and one or two appellate levels at the top. Cases originating in state courts ordinarily cannot be appealed to the federal courts unless a federal issue is involved, and then the federal courts can choose to rule only on the federal aspects of a case. Federal judges at all levels are nominated by the president and if confirmed by the Senate, they are appointed by the president to the office. Once on the federal bench, they serve until they die, retire or are removed by impeachment and conviction.

The Supreme Court is unquestionably the most important court in the country. Legal principles established by it are binding on lower courts and its capacity to define the law is enhanced by the control it exercises over the cases it hears. However, it is inaccurate to assume that lower courts are inconsequential (the upper-court myth). Lower courts have considerable discretion and a great majority of their decisions are not reviewed by higher courts. It is also inaccurate to assume that federal courts are far more significant than state courts (the federal court myth).

Courts have less discretionary authority than elected institutions. Judiciary positions are constrained by the facts of a case and by the laws as defined through the Constitution, statutes and government regulations, and legal precedent. Yet existing legal guidelines are seldom so precise that judges have no choice in their decisions. As a result, political influences have a strong impact on the judiciary. It responds to national conditions, public opinion, interest groups and elected officials, particularly the president and members of Congress. Another political influence on the judiciary is the personal beliefs of judges, who have individual preferences that are evident in the way they decide issues that come before them. Not surprisingly, partisan politics plays a significant role in judicial appointments.

In recent decades the Supreme Court has issued broad rulings on individual rights, some of which have required government to take positive action on behalf of minority interests. As the Court has crossed into areas traditionally left to lawmaking majorities, the legitimacy of its policies has been questioned. Advocates of judicial restraint claim that justices' personal values are inadequate justification for exceeding the proper judicial role. They argue that the Constitution entrusts broad public good issues to elective institutions and that judicial activism ultimately undermines public respect for the judiciary. Judicial activists counter that the courts were established as an independent branch and should not hesitate to promote new principles when they see a need, even if this action puts them into conflict with elected officials.

MAJOR CONCEPTS

appellate jurisdiction--the authority of a given court to review cases that have already been tried in lower courts and are appealed to it by the losing party; such a court is called an appeals court or appellate court.

compliance--the issue of whether a court's decisions will be respected and obeyed.

concurring opinion--a separate opinion written by a Supreme Court justice who votes with the majority on a case but who disagrees with their reasoning.

decision--a vote of the Supreme Court in a particular case that indicates which party the justices side with and by how large a margin.

dissenting opinion--the opinion of a justice in a Supreme Court case that explains the reasons for disagreeing with the majority position.

facts (of a court case)--the relevant circumstances of a legal dispute or offense as determined by a trial court. The facts of a case are crucial because they help to determine which law or laws are applicable in the case.

judicial activism--the doctrine that the courts should develop new legal principles when judges see a compelling need, even if this action places them in conflict with the policy decisions of elected officials.

judicial conference--a closed meeting of the justices of the U.S. Supreme Court to discuss the points of the cases before them; the justices are not supposed to discuss conference proceedings with outsiders.

judicial restraint--the doctrine that the judiciary should be highly respectful of precedent and should defer to the judgment of legislatures. The doctrine claims that the job of judges is to work within the confines of laws set down by tradition and law-making majorities.

jurisdiction (of a court)--a given court's authority to hear cases of a particular kind. Jurisdiction may be original or appellate.

laws (of a court case)--the constitutional provisions, legislative statutes or judicial precedents that apply to a court case.

legitimacy (of judicial power)--the issue of the proper limits of judicial authority in a political system based in part on the principle of majority rule.

majority opinion--a Supreme Court opinion that results when a majority of the justices are in agreement on the legal basis of a decision.

opinion (of a court)--a court's written explanation of its decision which serves to inform others of the legal basis for the decision. Supreme Court opinions are expected to guide the decisions of other courts.

original jurisdiction--the authority of a given court to be the first court to hear a case.

plurality opinion--a court opinion that results when a majority of justices agree on a decision in a case but do not agree on the legal basis for the decision. In such instances, the legal position held by most of the justices on the winning side is called a plurality opinion.

precedent--a judicial decision in a given case that serves as a rule of thumb for settling subsequent cases of a similar nature; courts are generally expected to follow precedent.

senatorial courtesy--the tradition that a U.S. senator from the state in which a federal judicial vacancy has arisen should have a say in the president's nomination of the new judge if the senator is of the same party as the president.

writ of *certiorari*-- permission granted by a higher court to allow a losing party in a legal case to bring the case before it for a ruling; when such a writ is requested of the U.S. Supreme Court, four of the Court's nine justices must agree to accept the case before it is granted *certiorari*.

BOXES, TABLES AND FIGURES IN THE TEXT

Boxes

      Types of Supreme Court Opinions
      States in the Nation: Principal Methods of Selecting State Judges
      How the U.S. Compares: Judicial Power
      Sources of Law That Constrain the Federal Judiciary's Decisions

Tables

      Justices of the Supreme Court, 1998
      Background Characteristics of Presidents' Judicial Nominees
      Significant Supreme Court Cases

Figures

      The Federal Judicial System

INTERNET RESOURCES

The Federal Court home page on the Web is located at: http://www.law.vill.edu/Fed-Ct/fedcourt.html

Charts to help in understanding the path and duties of federal courts can be accessed through: http://www.uscourts.gov/understanding_courts/899_toc.

Rules of the Supreme Court can be found at: http://www.law.cornell.edu/rules/supct/overview.html

Resumes and opinions of current Supreme Court justices can be found at: http://www.law.cornell.edu/supct/justices/fullcourt.html

The Legal Information Institute provides Supreme Court opinions since 1990 at http://www.law.cornell.edu/   Try also http://www.findlaw.com

Indiana University School of Law provides a virtual law library of law-related documents and resources at: http://www.law.indiana.edu/law/v-lib/lawindex.html

This web site allows you to take the facts of actual court cases, examine the law and the arguments, and then decide each case for yourself. It can be found at: http://www.courttversuscom/cases

The home page of the Federal Judicial Center, an agency created by Congress to conduct research and provide education on the federal judicial system can be reached at: http://www.fjc.gov

The University of Michigan maintains a web page that provides detailed information on the federal judicial system. It can be reached at: http://www.lib.umich.edu/libhome/Documents.center/fedjudi.html

A useful site that provides links to the Supreme Court, pending cases, the state court systems, and other subjects can be reached at: http://www.rominger.com/supreme.htm

ANALYTICAL THINKING EXERCISES

A. By looking at the box on "Judicial Power," find the U.S. and explain what is meant by the claim that U.S. courts are highly political compared with the courts of many other democracies.

B. From Table 14-2 on "Background Characteristics of Presidents' Judicial Nominees" note what characteristics were favored by which presidents. Speculate on whether these characteristics affected judicial decision making trends among various presidential administrations.

C. Use the analytical thinking format from Chapter One of this *Study Guide* to discuss the chapter reading "Judicial Interpretation" by William Brennan, Jr., at the end of Chapter Fourteen of the text.

TEST QUESTIONS FOR REVIEW

True/False

1. The Supreme Court is given both original and appellate jurisdiction by the U.S. Constitution.

2. A majority of the cases the Supreme Court hears come to it through its appellate jurisdiction.

3. In contrast to Supreme Court judges, federal judges can be appointed by the president without Senate approval.

4. Partisanship is no longer an important factor in the nomination of lower court judges by the president.

5. Congress may sometimes structure its debate on legislation in such a way as to make its intent clear to the courts and thus to influence subsequent court decisions on the legislation.

6. The Supreme Court is responsive to public opinion, although much less so than Congress or the president.

7. Advocates of judicial restraint contend that judicial policymaking weakens compliance with judicial rulings, and thus erodes the Court's legitimacy.

8. Advocates of judicial activism maintain that the courts should work closely within the confines of legislation and precedent, seeking to discover their application to specific cases, rather than searching for new principles.

9. The facts of a case are important in determining which laws are applied to the case.

10. The Chief Justice of the Supreme Court must be a member of the majority decision of the court in order for it to be valid.

Multiple Choice

1. A Supreme Court justice who votes with the majority but for different legal reasons than the other justices in the majority would likely write what type of opinion?
a. majority
b. minority
c. dissenting
d. concurring

2. Although federal district courts are theoretically bound by Supreme Court precedents, they sometimes deviate because of which of the following:
a. the facts of a case are seldom precisely the same as those of a similar case decided by the Supreme Court.
b. federal judges may misunderstand the Court's position.
c. the opinion of a Supreme Court case is sufficiently broad so that lower courts can reasonably interpret it in somewhat different ways.
d. b and c only.
e. a, b and c

3. The lowest level of the federal court system is the:
a. court of appeal.
b. highest level of the state courts.
c. district court.
d. justice of the peace.

4. The "Missouri Plan" applies to selection of judges at which level?
a. federal
b. state
c. military court
d. tax courts

5. The "federal court myth" overlooks the fact that:
a. most court cases arise under state law, not federal law.
b. nearly all cases that originate in state courts are never reviewed by federal court.
c. federal courts must normally accept the facts of a case as determined by a state court when reviewing its decision.
d. a and c only.
e. a, b and c.

6. Sources of law that constrain federal judiciary decisions include all **except** which one of the following:
a. dissenting opinions.
b. U.S. Constitution.
c. statutory law.
d. precedent.
e. judicial activism

7. Judicial restraint holds that courts should:
a. refrain from interpreting the meaning of the law.
b. avoid common law rulings.
c. never overturn precedent.
d. act cautiously in overruling the decisions of elected officials.

8. Judicial review is:
a. a court decision that prohibits action by the Supreme Court.
b. the power of the courts to decide whether a governmental institution has acted within its constitutional powers.
c. an act by the Supreme Court to move lower court cases directly into the high court under its original jurisdiction.
d. congressional action to overrule Supreme Court decisions.

9. The U.S. Supreme Court makes its decisions:
a. in a very quick turnaround time frame.
b. in open hearing with the lawyers to the cases present.
c. by polling the states' best judges.
d. by consulting the president beforehand.
e. in judicial conference.

10. When a court relies on precedent it is:
a. using a previous judicial decision as a rule for settling subsequent cases of a similar nature.
b. avoiding *stare decisis*.
c. unable to overrule a lower court decision.
d. deferring to the state legislature for redress of the issue.

11. Justices on the losing side of a case can write which type of opinion?
a. *certiorari*
b. majority
c. concurring
d. dissenting
e. plurality

12. When a group that is not a party to a case but that wants its concerns included in the case's outcome, it can file a brief called:
a. *amicus curiae*.
b. Brandeis.
c. *stare decisis*.
d. activist
e. *en banc*.

13. The Constitution gives Congress power over the Supreme Court to:
a. make the court a part of the executive branch.
b. eliminate the court's original jurisdiction.
c. refuse to implement court decisions.
d. rewrite legislation it feels the court has misinterpreted.
e. appoint the Chief Justice.

14. The doctrine of judicial activism would suggest that the Supreme Court:
1. totally disregards judicial precedent.
2. promotes governmental interference in people's lives.
3. should interpret the law to protect rights of individuals to achieve social justice.
4. protect people from unreasonable government interference in their lives.
a. 1 and 2.   b. 3 and 4.   c. only 4.   d. 2, 3, 4.   e. all the above.

15. What can influence major shifts in the U.S. Supreme Court's positions on broad issues?
a. changes in membership on the court.
b. political trends.
c. public opinion.
d. b and c only.
e. a, b and c.

Essays

1. Name the ways that the U.S. judiciary is restricted in deciding cases. How do these restrictions affect the legal environment?

2. Describe the ways that the American judiciary is not a majoritarian institution, including roadblocks the public has to overcome to have a major influence on a pressing judicial issue. Are you comfortable with the judiciary's elitist position in America's political system?

3. The way America's Supreme Court uses judicial review varies between judicial restraint and judicial activism. Discuss what both of these approaches seek to achieve in deciding legal issues.

4. Discuss the major differences between the judicial system of the United States and those of other democracies. Are there any aspects of the operations of the judicial power of the other democracies that you think would be beneficial for the U.S. to adopt?

ANSWER KEY

True/False

1. T	3. F	5. T	7. T	9. T
2. T	4. F	6. T	8. F	10. F

Multiple Choice

1. d	4. b	7. d	10. a	13. d
2. e	5. e	8. b	11. d	14. b
3. c	6. a	9. e	12. a	15. e

CHAPTER FIFTEEN
- ECONOMIC AND ENVIRONMENTAL POLICY -

LEARNING OBJECTIVES

After reading this chapter students should be able to:

1. Discuss the principles behind the concept of a regulated economy.
2. Explain general differences between the economic ideas of Adam Smith and Karl Marx.
3. Describe the differences between regulatory policies of efficiency and equity.
4. Explain the function of the Federal Trade Commission.
5. Distinguish between fiscal and monetary policy.
6. Distinguish between the general principles of supply-side and demand-side theories.
7. Discuss how deregulation serves the economy.
8. Describe the Federal Reserve System's role in America's economy.

FOCUS AND MAIN POINTS

This chapter examines the economic role of government, focusing on its promotion and regulation of economic interests and its fiscal and monetary policies. Directly or indirectly, the federal government is a party to almost every economic transaction in which Americans engage. Although private decisions by firms and individuals are the main force in the American economic system, these decisions are influenced by government policy. Washington seeks to maintain high productivity, employment, and purchasing power; regulates business practices that would otherwise harm the environment or result in economic inefficiencies and inequities; and promotes economic interests. The main ideas presented in the chapter are the following:

> Through regulation, the U.S. government imposes restraints on business activity that are designed to promote economic efficiency and equity.

Through regulatory and conservation policies, the U.S. government seeks to protect and preserve the environment from the effects of business firms and consumers.

Through promotion, the U.S. government helps private interests to achieve their economic goals.

Through its taxing and spending decisions (fiscal policy), the U.S. government seeks to maintain a level of economic supply and demand that will keep the economy prosperous.

Through its money-supply decisions (monetary policy), the U.S. government-- through the "Fed"--seeks to maintain a level of inflation   consistent with sustained controllable economic growth.

CHAPTER SUMMARY

Although private enterprise is the main force in America's economic system, the federal government plays a significant role through policies it selects to regulate, promote and stimulate the economy.

Regulatory policy is designed to achieve efficiency and equity, which require government to intervene, for example, in order to maintain competitive trade practices (an efficiency goal) and to protect vulnerable parties involved in economic transactions (an equity goal). Many of the regulatory decisions of the federal government, particularly those of older agencies, are made largely in a context of group politics. Business lobbies have an especially strong influence on regulatory policies that affect them. In general, newer regulatory agencies have policy responsibilities that are broader in scope and apply to a larger number of firms than those of older agencies. As a result, newer agency policy decisions are more often made in a party politics context. Republican administrations are less vigorous in their regulation of business than are Democratic administrations.

Business is a major beneficiary of federal government efforts that promote economic interests. A large number of programs, including those that provide loans and research grants, are designed to assist businesses, which are also protected from failure through such measures as tariffs and favorable tax laws. Labor, for its part, gets government assistance through laws concerning such matters as worker safety, the minimum wage and collective bargaining. Yet America's individualistic culture tends to put labor at a disadvantage, keeping it less powerful than business in its dealings with government. Agriculture is another economic sector that depends substantially on government's help, particularly in the form of income stabilization programs, such as those that provide subsidies and price supports.

The U.S. government pursues policies that are designed to protect and conserve the environment. A few decades ago, the environment was not a policy priority. Today, there are many programs in this area, and the public has become an active participant in efforts to conserve resources and prevent exploitation of the environment.

Through its fiscal and monetary policies, Washington attempts to maintain a strong and stable economy--one that is characterized by high productivity, high employment and low inflation. Fiscal policy is based on government decisions about spending and taxing, which are aimed at either stimulating a weak economy or dampening an overheated (inflationary) economy. Fiscal policy is worked out through Congress and the president and is consequently responsive to political pressures. However, since it is difficult to raise taxes or cut programs, government's ability to apply fiscal policy as an economic remedy is limited. Monetary policy is based on the money supply and works through the Federal Reserve System, which is headed by a board whose members hold office for fixed terms. The Fed is a relatively independent body, a fact that raises questions about whether it should have such a large role in national economic policy.

MAJOR CONCEPTS

balanced budget--revenues from taxes for the year were equal to government expenditures for that same year.

budget deficit--government expenditures for a given fiscal year exceed revenues from taxes.

budget surplus--occurs when the federal government receives more in tax and other revenues than it spends.

capital-gains tax--tax that individuals pay on gains in capital investments such as property and stock.

deficit-spending--spending for a given fiscal year exceeded revenues for that same year.

demand-side economics--a form of fiscal policy that emphasizes "demand" (consumer spending). Government can use increased spending or tax cuts to place more money in consumers' hands and thereby increase demand.
deregulation--rescinding regulations to improve efficiency.

economic depression--an exceptionally steep and sustained downturn in the economy.

economic recession--less severe downturn in the economy.

economy--a system of production and consumption of goods and services which are allocated through exchange among producers and consumers.

efficiency--the relationship of inputs (the labor and material that go into making   a product or service) to outputs (the product or service itself). The greater the output for a given input, the more efficient the production process.

equity (in relation to economic policy)--a situation in which the outcome of an economic transaction is fair to each party. An outcome can usually be considered fair if each party enters into a transaction freely and neither is at a disadvantage.

externalities--burdens that society incurs when firms fail to pay the full cost of resources used in production. An example of an externality is the pollution that results when corporations dump industrial wastes into lakes and rivers.

fiscal policy--a tool of economic management by which government attempts to maintain a stable economy through its taxing and spending decisions.

graduated personal income tax--tax rate goes up substantially as income rises.

inflation--an increase in the average level of prices of goods and services.

laissez-faire doctrine--a classic economic philosophy which holds that owners of businesses should be allowed to make their own production and distribution decisions without government regulation or control.

monetary policy--a tool of economic management available to government that involves manipulation of the amount of money in circulation.

national debt--the total amount owed to creditors by the federal government.

regulation--a term that refers to government restrictions on the economic practices of private firms.

supply-side economics--a form of fiscal policy that emphasizes "supply" (production). An example of supply-side economics would be a tax cut on business.

BOXES, TABLES AND FIGURES IN THE TEXT

Boxes
>How the U.S. Compares: Global Economic Competitiveness
>States in the Nation: Federal Taxing and Spending

Tables
>The Main Objectives of Regulatory Policy
>Fiscal Policy: A Summary
>Monetary Policy: A Summary

Figures
>The Federal Budget Dollar, Fiscal Year 2001
>Federal Budgetary Process
>The Federal Budget Deficit/Surplus, 1975-2009

INTERNET RESOURCES

The Federal Reserve Board can be located at: http://www.bog.frb.fed.us/

A copy of the federal budget and other economic data can be obtained at: http://www.whitehouse.gov/WH/EOP/omb.

A useful learning tool is a game about cutting the national budget. Playing the game illustrates the difficulties of setting economic priorities and working out differences. The game can be accessed at: http://www.i2020.net/~bsweb/jsydenst/usbudget.htm.

Another option for pursuing information about the budget and playing with altering it can be found at: http://star.catalog.com/budget/

Private research organizations can offer information on economic and other issues. The most comprehensive nonpartisan source is the Brookings Institution at: http://www.brook.edu.

A liberal source for information about economic issues is the Economic Policy Institute: http://epinet.org/.

A conservative source for information about economic issues can be found at the CATO Institute: http://www.cato.org/

The Environmental Protection Agency has information on environmental policy and regulations, EPA projects, and related subjects at: http://www.epa.gov

The Federal Trade Commission is one of the older regulatory agencies. Its web site describes the range of its activities at: http://www.ftc.gov

The home page of the Office of Management and Budget contains a summary of the annual federal budget and describes OMB's operations and responsibilities. It can be found at: http://www.whitehouse.gov/WH/EOP/OMB/html/ombhome.html

ANALYTICAL THINKING EXERCISES

A. Use the analytical thinking format at the beginning of Chapter One of this *Study Guide* to discuss the reading "Long-Term Goals for the Economy" by Alice Rivlin.

B. Look at Tables 15-2 and 15-3 and apply the principles presented in those tables to the following scenarios:

    1. Business is booming; worker employment is high; people have money and want to spend it; the stock market is climbing. What action can be taken to slow down business a little to keep inflation from eroding the gains?

    2. Business productivity is slowing and growth is below 2.5% per year. Corporations are downsizing and not only are less educated workers being laid off but middle management/college trained workers are also being laid off. What action can be taken to infuse growth into the economy?

TEST QUESTIONS FOR REVIEW

True/False

1. The economies of nearly all nations today are of a "mixed" form, meaning they include both free-market and collectivist elements.

2. The primary issue of government regulation is whether the costs to business outweigh potential benefits to society.

3. Interest groups do not attempt to bring pressure to bear on regulation of the economy.

4. Government intervenes to bring "equity" into the marketplace when, for example, it requires tobacco companies to place warnings about health risks related to smoking on cigarette packages.

5. In general, the economic policy pursued by the U.S. government has been harmful to business interests.

6. A government's fiscal policy is built on its taxing and spending decisions.

7. Monetary policy is controlled through the president and the executive branch.

8. In comparison with fiscal policy, monetary policy has at least one obvious advantage: it can be initiated more quickly because the Federal Reserve Board (the "Fed") is a faster-acting body than Congress.

9. When the Federal Reserve Board buys securities from the public, the effect that action has on the economy is to slow it down.

10. The U.S. Constitution says nothing about the economy.

11. The farm legislation of 1996 extended more farm subsidies to farmers than ever before in American history.

12. Rachel Carson's *Silent Spring* encouraged the growth of the modern environmental protection movement.

Multiple Choice

1. Trust-busting is an example of regulation to promote:
a. efficiency.
b. laissez-faire capitalism.
c. collectivism.
d. equity

2. The case of the Savings and Loan industry in America illustrates all **except** which one of the following:
a. excessive government regulation can make it difficult for firms to respond effectively to new economic conditions by burdening them with bureaucratic guidelines and costly implementation procedures.
b. the issue of business regulation is not a simple question of whether or not to regulate.
c. the challenge of regulation is to achieve the proper balance between government controls and free-market mechanisms.
d. private investors should be left completely in control of the economy since government intrusion infuses dishonesty into business practices.

3. The era of "New Social Regulation," which addressed issues such as the environment and worker safety, differed from the previous two eras of regulatory reform in that the:
a. Republican party took the lead in placing additional regulations on business.
b. aim was to regulate activities of firms of many types, not just those in a particular industry.
c. regulatory agencies were established in a way that prevented the president from having a role in their operations.
d. guiding principle was self-regulation: business was given wide leeway in deciding how it would comply with new requirements.

4. Government support for agriculture in the form of price supports and income subsidies:
a. increases farm production in order to meet the nation's food needs.
b. has been largely phased out by the 1996 Federal Agricultural Improvement and Reform Act (FAIR).
c. promote farm conservation in order to preserve the productive capacity of U.S. agriculture.
d. encourages rural development.

5. Keynesian economics emphasizes which of the following approaches as a means of curtailing economic downturns:
a. reduced taxes.
b. decreased government regulation.
c. increased government spending.
d. decreased inflation.

6. "Supply-side" economics was based primarily on:
a. stimulation of the business (supply) component.
b. government stimulation of consumer demands.
c. a repudiation of "trickle-down" theory.
d. increases in taxation.

7. The use of fiscal policy as an instrument for stimulating the economy has been restricted in recent years by:
a. emerging theories challenging the validity of the fiscal-policy model.
b. the conflicting fiscal-policy models employed by the Office of Management of Budget and the Congressional Budget Office.
c. the federal government's already large budget deficit, which has made it difficult for officials to increase spending as a means of encouraging economic growth.
d. Supreme Court decisions narrowing the fiscal authority of the national government.

8. The Federal Reserve Board is most directly charged with establishing which type of policy?
a. monetary
b. military
c. fiscal
d. budgetary

9. Monetary policy includes all of the following assumptions except:
a. control of the money supply is key to sustaining a healthy economy.
b. too little money in circulation contributes to inflation.
c. too little money in circulation contributes to a slowdown in consumer buying.
d. too little money in circulation contributes to a slowdown in production.

10. A major controversy surrounding the Federal Reserve's role in economic policy is:
a. the Fed's political accountability.
b. manipulation of the national economy.
c. the Fed's relationship to banking interests.
d. b and c only.
e. a, b and c.

11. Economic efficiency is measured by:
a. rejecting cost-benefit analysis of goods and services.
b. paying workers a wage above the value they add to production.
c. fulfilling as many of society's needs as possible while using as few of its resources as possible.
d. assuring free and fair economic transactions so all parties gain equally.

12. When customers do not pay all the costs that society has incurred in the production of goods and services, the unpaid costs are called:
a. economy.
b. externalities.
c. efficiency.
d. equities.

13. Government intervention in the economy occurs to:
1. stimulate the economy.
2. control inflation.
3. adjust the money supply.
4. address the national debt.
a. 1 and 2.   b. 3 and 4.   c. 1 and 4.   d. 2 and 3.   e. all the above.

14. The Democratic party would typically favor all **except** which one of the following economic policies when in office:
a. government spending to reduce inflation.
b. public jobs programs.
c. increased government spending for the employed.
d. increases in progressive tax rates for upper-income levels.

15. Government has aided labor over the years by legislating which of the following:
a. minimum wages and maximum work hour policies.
b. nondiscriminatory hiring practices.
c. unemployment benefits.
d. safer and more healthful working conditions.
e. all the above.

16. The purpose of Earth Day is to draw the public's attention to:
a. environmental issues.
b. deregulation of housing developers.
c. need to extend the dual use policy.
d. the space program.

17. Positive results from environmental regulation include which of the following:
a. improvement in air quality.
b. increased level of smog in cities.
c. improvement of water quality in some cities.
d. a and b.
e. a and c.

Essays

1. What phases of change has the American economic system gone through since the 1930s? What changes do you think are going to be the most important for the global economy in the next century?

2. How does government promote the interests of any two of the following: business, labor, agriculture?

3. Explain the differences between promoting the goals of economic efficiency and economic equity through government regulation of the economy.

4. Under which circumstances would fiscal policy be a more effective remedy for economic problems than monetary policy?

5. Identify two U.S. government policies that are designed to protect and conserve the environment. Evaluate their effectiveness.

ANSWER KEY

True/False

1. T	3. F	5. F	7. F	9. F	11. F
2. T	4. T	6. T	8. T	10. F	12. T

Multiple Choice

1. a	4. b	7. c	10. e	13. e	16. a
2. d	5. c	8. a	11. c	14. c	17. e
3. b	6. a	9. b	12. b	15. e	

CHAPTER SIXTEEN
- WELFARE AND EDUCATION POLICY -

LEARNING OBJECTIVES

After reading this chapter students should be able to

1. Define what "social welfare state" means.
2. Identify what the American poverty line entails.
3. Outline the development periods for America's welfare state.
4. Explain the major thrust of the 1996 Welfare Reform Act.
5. Identify what "entitlement" means.
6. Differentiate between social insurance and public assistance programs.
7. Explain what a transfer payment is.
8. Differentiate between the concepts of negative government and positive government
9. Explain Americans' attitudes towards equality of opportunity as applied to social welfare policy.

FOCUS AND MAIN POINTS

This chapter examines the social problems that federal welfare programs are designed to alleviate and describes how these programs operate. It addresses public education policy. A goal of this chapter is to provide an informed basis for understanding issues of social welfare and education and to show why disagreements in this area are so substantial. They involve making hard choices that almost inevitably require trade-offs between federal and state power and between the values of individual self-reliance and egalitarian compassion. The main points of the chapter are these:

Poverty is a large and persistent problem in America, affecting about one in seven Americans, including many of the country's most vulnerable groups--children, female-headed families, and minorities.

Welfare policy has been a partisan issue, with Democrats generally taking the lead on government programs to alleviate economic insecurity and Republicans acting to slow down or reverse these initiatives.

Social welfare programs are designed to reward and foster self-reliance or, when this is not possible, to provide benefits only to those individuals who are truly in need.

As a result of America's individualistic culture, public support for social insurance programs (such as social security) is far higher than for public assistance programs (such as TANF).

A prevailing principle in the United States is equality of opportunity, which in terms of public policy is most evident in the area of public education. No country invests more heavily in its public schools and colleges than does the United States.

CHAPTER SUMMARY

The United States has a complex social welfare system of multiple programs addressing specific welfare needs. Each program applies only to those individuals who qualify for benefits by meeting specific eligibility criteria. In general, these criteria are designed to reward and promote self-reliance or, when help is necessary, to ensure that laziness is not rewarded or fostered--in short, to limit benefits to those individuals who truly cannot help themselves. This approach to social welfare reflects Americans' traditional belief in individualism.

Poverty is a large and persistent problem in America. About one in seven people fall below the government-defined poverty line, and they include a disproportionate number of children, female-headed families, minority group members, and rural and inner-city dwellers. The ranks of the poor are increased by economic recessions and reduced through government welfare programs.

Welfare policy has been a partisan issue, with Democrats taking the lead on government programs to alleviate economic insecurity and Republicans acting to slow down or decentralize these initiatives. Changes in social welfare have usually occurred through presidential leadership in a context of majority support for change. Welfare policy has been implemented through programs to provide jobs and job training, education programs, income measures, and, especially, transfer payments through individual-benefit programs.

Individual-benefit programs fall into two broad categories: social insurance and public assistance. The former includes such programs as social security for retired workers and Medicare for the elderly. Social insurance programs are funded by payroll taxes on potential recipients, who thus, in a sense, earn the benefits they later receive. Because of this arrangement, social insurance programs have broad public support. Public assistance programs, in contrast, are funded by general tax revenues and are targeted toward needy individuals and families. These programs are not controversial in principle: most Americans believe that government should assist the truly needy. However, because of a widespread belief that most welfare recipients could get along without assistance if they tried, these programs do not have universal public support, are only modestly funded, and are politically vulnerable.

In its effort to create balance between economic equity on one hand and individualism on the other, the U.S. leans more heavily toward individualism than the other advanced industrialized democracies. Entitlement to social security, for example, is not a universal right of the elderly in the United States, whereas it is elsewhere. Compared with other democracies, however, the United States attempts to more equally educate its children, a policy consistent with its cultural emphasis on equality of opportunity.

The social welfare system in the United States is criticized in all quarters, but reform efforts have been largely unsuccessful. A major reason is that opposing sides disagree fundamentally on the nature of the problem. In one view, social welfare is too costly and assists too many people who could help themselves; another view holds that social welfare is not broad enough and that too many disadvantaged Americans live in poverty. In light of these differences, in combination with federalism and the widely shared view that welfare programs should target specific problems, the existing system of multiple programs, despite its administrative complexity and inefficiency, has been the only politically feasible alternative. Yet it results in social spending that is not fully targeted toward the people most in need of help.

MAJOR CONCEPTS

entitlement programs--individual-benefit programs, such as social security, that require government to provide a designated benefit to any person who meets the legally defined criteria for eligibility.

equality of opportunity--the idea that all individuals should be given an equal chance to succeed on their own.

in-kind benefit--a government benefit that is a cash equivalent, such as food stamps or rent vouchers. This form of benefit ensures that recipients will use public assistance in a specified way.

means test--the requirement that applicants for public assistance must demonstrate they are poor in order to be eligible for assistance.

negative government--the philosophical belief that government governs best by staying out of people's lives, thus giving individuals as much freedom as possible to determine their own pursuits.

positive government--the philosophical belief that government intervention is necessary in order to enhance personal liberty when individuals are buffeted by economic and social forces beyond their control.

poverty line--as defined by the federal government, the poverty line is the annual cost of a thrifty food budget for an urban family of four, multiplied by three to allow also for the cost of housing, clothes and other expenses. Families below the poverty line are considered poor and are eligible for certain forms of public assistance.

public assistance--a term that refers to social welfare programs funded through general tax revenues and available only to the financially needy. Eligibility for such programs is established through a means test.

social insurance--social welfare programs based on the "insurance" concept, so that individuals must pay into the program in order to be eligible to receive funds from it. An example is social security for retired people.

transfer payment--a government benefit that is given directly to an individual, as in the case of social security payments to a retiree.

BOXES, TABLES AND FIGURES IN THE TEXT

Boxes
>	How the U.S. Compares: Children Living in Poverty
>	States in the Nation: Families on Welfare

Figures
>	Percentage of Families Living in Poverty, By Family Composition and Race/Ethnicity
>	Income Inequality
>	The Cumbersome Administrative Process By Which Welfare Recipients Get Their Benefits
>	Federal Spending For Social Insurance and Public Assistance Programs

INTERNET RESOURCES

For a wide range of information relating to domestic policy, consult the Electronic Policy Network at : http://epn.org.

For information on Medicare and Medicaid, see http://www.hcfa.gov.

Information about social security can be obtained at: http://www.ssa.gov.

Information about welfare reform can be found at: http://www.urban.org/welfare/overview.htm.

Consult the U.S. Department of Labor's web site for the status of the Welfare-to-Work program, including state-by-state assessments at: http://www.doleta.gov

The National Education Association has a home page that provides information on the organization's membership and policy goals. It can be reached at: http://www.nea.org

The web site of the Department of Health and Human Services can be located at: http://www.os.dhhs.gov

The University of Michigan's Program on Poverty and Social Welfare Policy maintains a web site that seeks to stimulate interest in policy issues and to

transmit research findings to policy makers. It can be accessed at:
http://www.ssw.umich.edu/poverty/mission.html

ANALYTICAL THINKING EXERCISES

A. Find Figure 16-2 in your text and look at the array of income inequalities that exist in the United States. Describe the ratio of rich to poor in the U.S. by looking at which percentage of the public receive which levels of income. What percent of total national income is received by the bottom 20 percent of people? What percent of total national income is receive by the top 5% of people in the U.S.? Are you comfortable with the gap between these two sectors and the knowledge that the gap is widening?

B. Look at Figure 16-4 in your text and answer the following questions about information contained in it: a) what forms of federal welfare spending are the most costly? b) does the data presented in this figure support the claim that welfare does not go to the truly needy? c) did the information from this table present a new perspective to what you already knew about federal spending?

C. Use the analytical thinking format from Chapter One of this *Study Guide* to discuss the reading "Saving Social Security" by Robert Reischauer. How does information presented in this article square with that presented in Chapter Sixteen?

TEST QUESTIONS FOR REVIEW

True/False

1. About one in seven Americans live at or below the poverty line.

2. "Feminization of poverty" reflects the fact that most Americans below the poverty line are members of single-mother families.

3. A higher percentage of white Americans live below the poverty line than Hispanics and African Americans.

4. The term "means test" refers to a tax on part of the social security income of wealthier retirees.

5. The major difference between social insurance programs and public assistance programs is that social insurance programs are available only to the financially needy.

6. Social insurance programs enjoy a greater degree of support among the American public than public assistance programs.

7. A plan for a guaranteed annual income has been proposed in the U.S. by both liberals and conservatives in order to help streamline the size and complexity of the welfare bureaucracy.

8. The United States ranks first in the world in the proportion of adults receiving a college education.

9. No one in the United States lives in poverty.

10. The U.S. government spends much less on public housing than on tax breaks for homeowners, most of whom are middle-and upper-income Americans.

11. Congressional support for large appropriations for aid to poorer schools is one of the easier measures to get approved in Congress.

12. In the U.S. education is primarily a federal rather than a state and local responsibility.

Multiple Choice

1. The poverty line for Americans is defined as:
a. the annual cost of all goods and services that a person can reasonably be expected to need.
b. the line below which ten percent of American people live.
c. the annual cost of a thrifty food budget for an urban family of four, multiplied by three.
d. an income of less than $10,000 per person.

2. According to survey data, the form of assistance that Americans favor most to help the poor is:
a. cash grants to poor families.
b. education and job training.
c. government jobs through government programs.
d. government services for the poor.

3. The leading social insurance program is:
a. unemployment insurance.
b. social security for retirees.
c. Medicare.
d. public assistance programs such as food stamps.

4. Social insurance programs have high levels of public support largely because:
a. of their self-financing feature.
b. they are based on an equality principle--all citizens are eligible for the benefits and all recipients receive the same level of benefits.
c. their cost is consistently below the spending level for public assistance programs.
d. they create an economic surplus for government to use for other programs.

5. Of the following, which is probably the least criticized public assistance program?
a. Supplemental Security Income
b. Aid to Families with Dependent Children (pre-TANF)
c. Food Stamps
d. Medicaid

6. Most social welfare programs are:
a. uniform throughout the states.
b. widely supported by Americans.
c. run jointly by federal and state governments.
d. managed entirely by the federal government.

7. The U.S. welfare system is "inefficient" in the sense that:
a. not enough money is available to support all eligible applicants.
b. too much political infighting occurs in Congress to ever achieve
 . significant welfare reform.
c. too much money is spent on individuals who are able-bodied but simply prefer not to work.
d. a large portion of the welfare budget never reaches the people it is intended to help, but is instead spent on the large bureaucracy that is required to administer the programs.

8. "Inequity" in the U.S. welfare system describes the fact that:
a. many people who need public assistance cannot qualify for it because the eligibility rules are so arbitrary.
b. the public thinks that most welfare recipients are minority-group members, while in fact most recipients are white.
c. most able-bodied people would be better off economically if they were on welfare than if they were working.
d. the people who are more in need of welfare get less assistance from government than the people who are less in need.

9. Today, the government standard for the poverty line is approximately how much for a family of four?
a. $8,500 per year
b. $10,500 per year
c. $16,700 per year
d. $28,500 per year

10. When government gives a benefit directly to an individual such as in the form of a check made out in their name, it is called what kind of payment?
a. government voucher
b. food stamps
c. in-kind benefits
d. transfer payment
e. subsidy payment

11. Which concept of government maintains that government intervention is necessary in order to enhance personal liberty and security?
a. pro-active government
b. transfer of responsibility
c. positive government
d. negative government
e. socialism

12. Medicaid is available to:
a. any American who needs medical care.
b. all Americans at least 62 years old.
c. people who are already on welfare.
d. anyone who cannot afford health insurance.

13. Americans tend to favor:
a. a guaranteed annual income for every American family.
b. reduction of welfare expenditures.
c. labor intensive welfare policies to make sure that people getting benefits really need them.
d. a and b only.
e. b and c only.

14. The 1996 Welfare Reform Act that passed Congress provides:
a. an end to the federal guarantee of cash assistance to needy families.
b. for cash grants to states who must take responsibility for welfare recipients.
c. a limitation of five years for a person to receive welfare.
d. that states must help welfare recipients find employment.
e. all the above.

15. Regarding income and tax measures in the United States, one can state that:
a. there are wide disparities in the income of those individuals at the top and the bottom of the income ladder.
b. income taxes in the U.S. have not been the instrument of redistribution that they are in other democracies.
c. through the Earned Income Tax Credit, the top 10% of tax payers can keep more than half of the tax money they owe.
d. a and b only.
e. a, b and c.

16. Recent concerns among Americans about public education relate to:
a. violence in schools.
b. level of pay and work load for teachers.
c. the ability to choose the school one's children will attend.
d. b and c.
e. a and c.

17. Which sector of American society has played the largest role in creating an equal opportunity society:
a. private enterprise.
b. the defense establishment.
c. government public assistance programs.
d. public education.

Essays

1. In the United States there is a great need for public assistance programs such as job training and aid for families with dependent children, for example, yet most money goes to social security, Medicare and the top fifth of those in the income population. What, if any, changes do you think will have to occur in order for those who need the assistance the most to really receive it?

2. Social welfare policy differences between the United States and European democracies stem from cultural and historical differences. Explain what these are and how they have affected the role of government in providing public assistance.

3. Summarize the changes in aid to needy families made in the 1996 Welfare Reform Act. Speculate on how you think these changes will impact people in your state, including some plans that your state has made to implement the act.

4. Differentiate between a social insurance program and a public assistance program, giving examples and a critical evaluation of each.

5. What are the pros and cons of the school choice issue?

6. If public schools have played such an important role in creating an equal opportunity society in the U.S., why would people want to criticize them?

ANSWER KEY

True/False

1. T	3. F	5. F	7. T	9. F	11. F
2. T	4. F	6. T	8. T	10. T	12. F

Multiple Choice

1. c	4. a	7. d	10. d	13. e	16. e
2. b	5. a	8. d	11. c	14. e	17. d
3. b	6. c	9. c	12. c	15. d	

CHAPTER SEVENTEEN
- FOREIGN AND DEFENSE POLICY -

LEARNING OBJECTIVES

After reading this chapter students should be able to:

1. Identify what national security policy is.
2. Distinguish between major aspects of foreign and defense policy before and after the cold war.
3. Differentiate between an isolationist and an internationalist foreign policy.
4. Define multilateralism and identify the instruments used to engage in it.
5. Identify the key policy-making actors in U.S. foreign and defense policy.
6. Explain at least four out of the six types of military action for which U.S. military forces have been trained.
7. Identify the concept and components of the military-industrial complex.
8. Describe the opposing arguments of protectionism and free trade.
9. Identify what foreign assistance (aid) is, how much the U.S. spends, and for what general purposes.

FOCUS AND MAIN POINTS

The national security policies of the U.S. are complex and varied, encompassing military, diplomatic and economic relations with some 160 nations around the world. This chapter focuses on the roots of U.S. foreign and defense policy, the process of foreign and military policymaking and the military and economic dimensions of national security policy. The main points the chapter makes are:

Since World War II, the United States has acted as world leader, a role that has substantially affected its military, diplomatic and economic policies.

The United States maintains a high degree of defense preparedness, which mandates a substantial level of defense spending and a worldwide deployment of U.S. conventional and strategic forces.

Changes in the international marketplace have led to increased economic interdependence among nations, which has had a marked influence on the U.S economy and on security planning. Increasingly, national security has been defined in economic rather than military terms.

CHAPTER SUMMARY

From 1948 to 1991, U.S. foreign and defense policies were dominated by concern about the Soviet Union. During most of this period the United States pursued a policy of containment based on the premise that the Soviet Union was an aggressor nation bent on global conquest. Containment policy led the United States into wars in Korea and Vietnam and led to development of a large defense establishment. U.S. military forces are deployed around the globe, and the nation has a large nuclear arsenal. The end of the cold war, however, has made some of this weaponry and much of the traditional military strategy less relevant to maintaining America's security. Cutbacks in military spending and a redefinition of the military's role are under way.

With the end of the cold war the United States has taken a new approach to foreign affairs, which President George Bush labeled as a "new world order." It proposes that nations work together toward common goals and includes efforts to address global problems, such as drug trafficking and environmental pollution. The Persian Gulf war is the most notable example of the multilateralism that is a characteristic of the new world order.

Increasingly, national security is being defined in economic terms. After World War II, the United States helped establish a global trading system within which it was the leading partner. The nation's international economic position, however, has gradually weakened owing to domestic problems and to the emergence of strong competitors, particularly Japan and Germany. Many analysts believe that a revitalized economic sector rather than military power holds the key to America's future position in international affairs.

The chief instruments of national security policy are diplomacy, military force, economic exchange and intelligence gathering. These are exercised through specialized agencies of the U.S. government, such as the Departments of State and Defense, which are largely responsive to presidential leadership. Increasingly, national security policy has also relied on international organizations, such as the UN and WTO, which are responsive to the global concerns of major nations.

MAJOR CONCEPTS

<u>cold war</u>--the lengthy period after World War II when the United States and the USSR were not engaged in actual combat (a "hot war") but were nonetheless locked in a state of deep-seated hostility.

<u>containment</u>--a doctrine developed after World War II based on the assumptions that the Soviet Union was an aggressor nation and that only a determined United States could block Soviet territorial ambitions.

<u>detente</u>--a French word meaning "a relaxing" used to refer to an era of improved relations between the U.S. and the Soviet Union that began in the early 1970s.

<u>deterrence</u>-the idea that nuclear war can be discouraged if each side in a conflict has the capacity to destroy the other with nuclear weapons.

<u>economic globalization</u>--the increased interdependence of nations' economies as a result of the impact of the transportation and communication revolutions on how business firms conduct their operations.

<u>free trade</u>--the view that all countries benefit to the degree that trade between them is not impeded by tariffs and other forms of protectionism.

<u>insurgency</u>--a type of military conflict in which irregular soldiers rise up against an established regime.

<u>internationalism</u>--the view that the country should involve itself deeply in world affairs.

<u>isolationism</u>--the view that the country should deliberately avoid a large role in world affairs and, instead, concentrate on domestic concerns.

<u>military-industrial complex</u>--the three components (the military establishment, the industries that manufacture weapons, and the members of Congress from states and districts that depend heavily on the arms industry) that mutually benefit from a high level of defense spending.

<u>multilateralism</u>--the situation in which nations act together in response to problems and crises.

multinational corporations--business firms that have significant operations in more than one country.

protectionism--the view that the immediate interests of domestic producers should have a higher priority (through, for example, protective tariffs) than free trade among nations.

BOXES, TABLES AND FIGURES IN THE TEXT

Boxes
   How the U.S. Compares: The Burden of Military Spending
   States in the Nation: Foreign Exports and State Economies
Table
   U.S. Assistance to Developing Countries
Figures
   The Trade Deficit
   Per Capita Assistance to Developing Countries

INTERNET RESOURCES

Information about the political science fields of international relations and comparative politics can be obtained through the American Political Science Association Gopher. Try gopher://apsa.trenton.edu:70/

The U.S. State Department can be accessed at: http://www.state.gov/

The CIA can be accessed at: http://www.odci.gov/cia/

General information about foreign affairs can be obtained from http://www.pitt.edu:81/~ian/ianframe.htm or from the Brookings Institution at http://www.brook.edu.

Information about the European Union can be found at: http://europa.eu.int/

The U.S. Commerce Department provides information on emerging markets through: http://www.stat-usa.gov/itabems.html.

The U.S. Department of Defense's web site provides information on each of the armed services, daily news from the American Forces Information Service, and other material. It can be located at: http://www.defenselink.mil

For reports and assessments of the Council of Foreign Relations and transcripts of speeches by U.S. and world political leaders on topics of international interest see: http://www.foreignrelations.org

The Institute for Global Communications provides information and services to organizations and activists on a broad range of international issues including human rights. It can be found at: http://www.igc.org/igc

The World Trade Organization web site contains information on the organization's activities and has links to related sites at: http://www.wto.org

ANALYTICAL THINKING EXERCISE

A. Use the analytical thinking format found in Chapter One of this *Study Guide* to discuss "A Borderless World" by Kenichi Ohmae at the end of Chapter Seventeen in your text.

TEST QUESTIONS FOR REVIEW

True/False

1. The major lesson of Munich was that appeasement policy works and is a good model for multilateralism.

2. U.S. national security policy after World War II was built chiefly upon a concern with the power and intentions of the Soviet Union.

3. Nearly everyone agrees that the U.S. could have won the Vietnam War with the use of sufficient military force.

4. "Detente" refers to the new era of the U.S.-Soviet communication and cooperation that began when it became clear that the United States would not win the Vietnam War.

5. The object of deterrence was to assure an American victory over the Soviet Union during a full-scale nuclear war.

6. The Central Intelligence Agency (CIA) has recently given greater attention to such problems as drug trafficking, industrial espionage and terrorism.

7. The United States prefers to define free trade and deliver its own economic assistance rather than work through agencies such as IMF and GATT.

8. The end of the Cold War has reduced the likelihood of unlimited conventional war.

9. U.S. national security policy has increasingly included a concern for the country's economic strength.

10. The U.S. spends more on foreign aid as a percentage of its total federal budget than most other democracies.

Multiple Choice

1. In his post World War II analysis of Soviet foreign policy aims, George Kennan recommended:
a. appeasement of Soviet military ambitions.
b. military intervention to overthrow the Soviet government.
c. adoption of a policy of detente.
d. containment of the USSR as a regional aggressor nation.

2. The Marshall Plan
a. financed the overthrow of nations with Communist governments.
b. proposed fourteen points for world peace, based on self-determination of all peoples.
c. proposed the alliance system known as NATO.
d. invested billions of American dollars in the rebuilding of Western European economies after World War II.

3. The idea that major nations should act together in response to problems and crises is called:
a. unilateralism.
b. detente.
c. multilateralism.
d. containment.

4. For the most balanced assessment of foreign and military policy issues, the president in most instances would be advised to follow the recommendations of the:
a. Department of State.
b. Department of Defense.
c. National Security Council.
d. Joint Chiefs of Staff.

5. The policy of deterrence, which the United States followed during the cold war, is based on the idea that:
a. the best protection against attack by an enemy is the capacity to retaliate with a devastating attack of one's own.
b. when threatened, a nation should strike first so that its enemy is deprived of the option of a surprise attack.
c. economic links with another country will deter it from aggression.
d. modern warfare requires a nation to follow a "flexible response" policy.

6. The fundamental cause for insurgency in most Third World countries has been:
a. grievances against economically and politically-powerful ruling elites.
b. the ideological rivalry between communism and capitalism.
c. rising levels of nationalism in reaction to the economic and political influence of foreign corporations.
d. destruction of the environment.

7. Broad U.S. goals in the global economy include:
a. sustaining an open system of trade that will promote domestic prosperity.
b. maintaining access to energy and other vital resources.
c. keeping the widening gap between the rich and poor countries from destabilizing the world's economy.
d. b and c only.
e. a, b and c.

8. As an instrument of U.S. economic policy, military force:
a. has become more important because of the threat of international terrorism to the free flow of U.S. goods.
b. has become more important because rising ethnic tensions are disrupting the creation of new markets for U.S. goods.
c. has become less important because the world economy is now so interconnected that the use of military force would probably be more disruptive than helpful.
d. has become less important because it places too heavy a drain on an already straining economy.

9. The *lesson of Vietnam* for the United States was that:
a. America's military arsenal was obsolete and needed updating.
b. appeasement only encourages further aggression.
c. there were limits to America's ability to assert its will in the world alone.
d. an isolationist foreign policy is the only safe direction for U.S. policy.

10. The chief instruments of national security policy include all except which one of the following:
a. reconstruction.
b. diplomacy.
c. military force.
d. economic exchange.
e. intelligence gathering.

11. Which type of military action is most likely to be used today?
a. limited nuclear warfare.
b. police-type action.
c. unlimited conventional warfare.
d. counterinsurgency.

12. The changing post-cold war world economy has impacted the U.S. by:
1. vaulting the U.S. to global economic dominance.
2. weakening the position of the U.S. in the world economy.
3. enabling Japan and Germany to become leading economic powers.
4. reducing the economic strength of the European Union.
a. 1 and 2.   b. 1 and 3.   c. 2 and 3.   d. 3 and 4.   e. only 1.

13. Approximately what percent of the U.S. federal budget is devoted to foreign aid:
a. less than 1 percent.
b. 10 percent.
c. 25 percent.
d. more than 30 percent.

14. Foreign investment by U.S.-based multinational corporations works to America's advantage in at least two of which of the following important ways:
1. increases inflation since the U.S. dollar fluctuates on the open market.
2. decreases the U.S. debt since it means that the U.S. imports more than it exports.
3. sends a flow of overseas profits back to the U.S. which strengthens the U.S. financial base.
4. makes other nations that are dependent on U.S. prosperity link their economic health to that of U.S. business.
a. 1 and 2.   b. 2 and 4.   c. 1 and 4.   d. 3 and 4.   e. 2 and 3.

15. Which is the most important of America's military alliances?
a. NORAD
b. DOT
c. NATO
d. IMF

Essays

1. Explain what a policy of multilateralism entails. What are some of the forces that encourage its pursuit and what are the cautionary aspects of this policy?

2. Describe some of the changes that have occurred in U.S. foreign policy since the collapse of the Soviet Union.

3. Describe the broad goals that the U.S. wants to pursue in the global economy. How do multinational corporations fit into the pursuit of these goals?

4. Since the United States is a democracy with a strong tradition of civil rights, do you think that economic growth and opening of new markets should take a back seat in foreign policy to establishment of civil rights protections within nations that are prospective trading partners?

ANSWER KEY

True/False

1. F	3. F	5. F	7. F	9. T
2. T	4. T	6. T	8. T	10. F

Multiple Choice

1. d	4. c	7. e	10. a	13. a
2. d	5. a	8. c	11. b	14. d
3. c	6. a	9. c	12. c	15. c

Notes

Notes

Notes

Notes

Notes

Notes

Notes

Notes

Notes

Notes